Islam

A SHORT INTRODUCTION

OTHER BOOKS IN THIS SERIES:

Buddhism: A Short History, Edward Conze, ISBN 1–85168–221–X
Buddhism: A Short Introduction, Klaus K. Klostermaier, ISBN 1–85168–186–8
Hinduism: A Short History, Klaus K. Klostermaier, ISBN 1–85168–213–9
Hindu Writings: A Short Introduction to the Major Sources, Klaus K. Klostermaier, ISBN 1–85168–230–9
Hinduism: A Short Introduction, Klaus K. Klostermaier, ISBN 1–85168–220–1
Islamic Philosophy, Theology and Mysticism: A Short Introduction, Majid Fakhry, ISBN 1–85168–252–X
Muhammad: A Short Biography, Martin Forward, ISBN 1–85168–131–0
Islam: A Short History, William Montgomery Watt, ISBN 1–85168–205–8
Jesus Christ: A Short Biography, Martin Forward, ISBN 1–85168–172–8
Christianity: A Short Introduction, Keith Ward, ISBN 1–85168–229–5
Judaism: A Short History, Lavinia and Dan Cohn-Sherbok, ISBN 1–85168–206–6
Judaism: A Short Introduction, Lavinia and Dan Cohn-Sherbok, ISBN 1–85168–207–4
Judaism: A Short Reader, Lavinia and Dan Cohn-Sherbok, ISBN 1–85168–112–4
A Short Introduction to the Old Testament Prophets, E. W. Heaton, ISBN 1–85168–114–0
Sufism: A Short Introduction, William C. Chittick, ISBN 1–85168–211–2
The Bahá'í Faith: A Short Introduction, Moojan Momen, ISBN 1–85168–209–0
The Bahá'í Faith: A Short History, Peter Smith, ISBN 1–85168–208–2
The Psychology of Religion: A Short Introduction, Kate M. Loewenthal, ISBN 1–85168–212–0
Confucianism: A Short Introduction, John and Evelyn Berthrong, ISBN 1–85168–236–8
Pluralism in the World Religions: A Short Introduction, Harold Coward, ISBN 1–85168–243–0
Global Philosophy of Religion: A Short Introduction, Joseph Runzo, ISBN 1–85168–235–X

RELATED TITLES PUBLISHED BY ONEWORLD:

What Muslims Believe, John Bowker, ISBN 1–85168–169–8
The Qur'án and its Exegesis, Helmut Gätje, ISBN 1–85168–118–3
The Faith and Practice of Al-Ghazali, William Montgomery Watt, ISBN 1–85168–062–4
On Being a Muslim, Farid Esack, ISBN 1–85168–146–9
Revival and Reform in Islam, Fazlur Rahman, edited and with an introduction by Ebrahim Moosa, ISBN 1–85168–204–X
Qur'án, Liberation and Pluralism, Farid Esack, ISBN 1–85168–121–3

Islam

A SHORT INTRODUCTION

Signs, symbols and values

Abdulkader Tayob

ONEWORLD
OXFORD

ISLAM: A SHORT INTRODUCTION

Oneworld Publications
(Sales and Editorial)
185 Banbury Road
Oxford OX2 7AR
England
http://www.oneworld-publications.com

Oneworld Publications
(US Marketing Office)
160 N. Washington St.
4th floor, Boston
MA 02114
USA

Reprinted 2000

A CIP record for this title is available
from the British Library

ISBN 1–85168–192–2

Cover design by Design Deluxe, Bath
Photographs pp. 17 and 116 from Peter Sanders Photography, High Wycombe
Typeset by LaserScript, Mitcham
Printed and bound in England by Clays Ltd, St Ives plc

CONTENTS

FIGURES

PREFACE

The presence of so many good introductions to Islam calls for justification for yet another book. This introduction does not propose to replace all previous attempts at introducing a complex and multi-faceted subject. Rahman's scholarly *Islam (*1979), Esposito's extensively informative *Islam: The Straight Path*, and Martin's insightful *Islamic Studies: A History of Religions Approach* (1996) are my immediate recommendations to students who are looking for relevant introductory materials. These texts, each in its own manner and through its own methodology, approach the subject with erudition, sensitivity and great insight. They are a welcome sight in a field that abounds with misconceptions and prejudice. In my view, these and other good introductions will satisfy the specific needs of individuals.

My own experience as teacher of an introductory course in Islam has taught me that students are also looking for direct access to the material and tangible aspects of the religion of Islam. Rather than first appreciating life in Arabia before the advent of Islam, they want to understand and appreciate the significance of a minaret, the reason why Muslims must wash before prayer, and the spiritual meaning of *ḥajj*. These queries often do not seek answers involving lengthy historical background and details of social evolution. The search for more extensive information and background may come later, but the immediate need is for understanding in the midst of the negative images associated with Islam, or simply from an encounter with a friend. As a result, I have written this book with the idea that the visible and apparent call is for explanation and understanding. In the process, I have dipped extensively into both the experiences of Islam and the scholarly contributions to debates and issues.

The book leads the reader into Islam by walking him or her through a mosque. It is a somewhat meandering tour, based on the principle that the immediate object or concept calls for attention and explication. Beginning with the minaret and ending with the *minbar* (pulpit), it uses the structures of a mosque to wander through the rich and fascinating images, symbols and values of Islam. It begins with the tangible and quickly moves to the intangible and abstract, and back again. Social significance is not far behind an exploration of how Muslims use and grapple with the challenges of their faith and tradition. Each of the key structures of the mosque is used to explore other, seemingly unrelated, aspects of Islam. Thus, for example, the minaret calls attention to the significance of height in Islamic architecture, but also to the presence of Islam among other religious traditions, the issue of music in Muslim society and the place of modern technology in Islamic rituals. I have avoided the tendency to oversimplify the complex questions concerning religion in the modern world. Thus, in almost every case, the book explores and informs, but also grapples with the familiar and commonplace. In my research for this book, I have come across aspects of Islamic history of which I was unaware, and I share these with the reader. This introduction is simply not an introductory gloss on Islam but, hopefully, a challenging encounter.

The best way to read this book is to start from the beginning and allow me to lead you through the mosque. If it happens that I have assumed too much in the first chapter, then use the index to find a quick explanation of a concept or term. I hope that this does not happen too often as I have carefully mapped the topics from chapter to chapter. On the other hand, you may begin with the index and use the text to focus on short introductions to *Sharīʻah* (jurisprudence), inter-religious dialogue, *ḥadīth* (statements of the Prophet) and its criticism, leadership, Sunnism, Shiʻism and many other issues. These topics are embedded within the discussion, but they may also be read about on their own.

Finally, it is pleasure to acknowledge the help and assistance of many of my friends and family and of institutions without whom the work would not have been completed. I would like to thank Novin Doostdar of Oneworld Publications for his invitation to write this work and faith in my ability to do so. The Department of Religious Studies at the University of Virginia deserves credit for providing computer, Internet and other technological facilities during my sabbatical in the spring semester of 1998 (South Africa's autumn, I might add). Students at both the University of Cape Town and the University of Virginia have been my guinea pigs in the writing of such a book. Their questions and queries, as well as their receptiveness to my attempts to answer, have shaped this book. A circle of friends at the University of Virginia encouraged me with their comments. I would like specifically to mention Kandioura Drame, Cindy Hohler-Fatton, Adam Gaiser, Shahriyar Muazzam Khan, Wali Ahmad, Ali Sachedina, Faraydoon Hovaizi, Shahnaaz Ghassemi, and Abdul Aziz Sachedina. Last but not least, my wife Hawa and children Shaheed, Huda and Tahseen make all this worthwhile, and without them this text would be so much the poorer.

NOTE ON DATES, TRANSLITERATION AND TRANSLATIONS

It is important to remember that Muslims use a unique *hijrī* calendar beginning with the emigration of the Prophet from Mecca to Medina in 622 CE, and based on lunar cycles. This introductory book, however, will only provide the corresponding Gregorian year. The transliteration of non-English terms follows the conventions of the *International Journal for Middle Eastern Studies*. I have used both Yusuf Ali's and Muhammad Asad's translations of the Qur'ān (Ali, *The Holy Qur'ān*, Washington, DC: Amanah Corporation, 1989; Asad, *The Message of the Qur'ān*, Gibraltar: Dar al-Andalus, 1980), sometimes modified for more contemporary syntax where I felt this was necessary. Translations of *ḥadith* are my own where no other English translation is cited.

1 THE MINARET
The call of Islam

> Ibn 'Umar, the son of the second caliph of Islam, used to say: When the people came to Medina, they would meet for worship without anybody calling them together. Then, one day, they discussed this and some suggested that they use a bell like the Christians. Others said that they should use a bugle like the Jews. But 'Umar said: Would you not send a person who would call others for prayer? And the Messenger of God said: Bilāl, stand up and give the call to prayer.
>
> (Ibn Ḥajar n.d.: II, 77)

Bilāl climbed on the roof and announced the following call to prayer in his most beautiful voice:

> God is Great (twice)
> I testify that there is no deity but God (twice)
> I testify that Muhammad is the Messenger of God (twice)
> Come to worship (twice)
> Come to success (twice)
> God is Great (twice)
> There is no deity but God

There is something slightly ironic in Bilāl, a former African slave, being the first caller in Islam. Bilāl was one of the first persons to accept Muhammad as the Prophet of God. As a slave, his decision to accept the new religion was opposed by his owner, who exposed him to inhuman torture and abuse. Like many religions, Islam was opposed by the beneficiaries of the status quo. At times Bilāl was placed on the hot sands of the Arabian desert, and forced to recant his faith. A model of steadfastness and faith, Bilāl responded to his tormenter with the singular word *aḥad* (one) in reference to his belief in the one supreme God. When the new faith was established through this call to prayer, Bilāl's announcement of the unity of God was a poignant statement to his erstwhile persecutors. The people of Mecca, unwilling to accept the unity of God, had been unable to suppress Bilāl's faith. Now, a few years later, the erstwhile downtrodden slave was boldly announcing that same message in Medina. The call to prayer in Islam is certainly a rousing call to humankind, which continues to be heard throughout the world. Every time Muslims hear it, it conjures up the symbol of Bilāl's call to the world in pre-Islamic Arabia.

This is one of a number of accounts of how the call to prayer originated in Islam. As a visible symbol which announces the presence of Islam, the call to prayer may be fruitfully explored from a number of perspectives. We will begin with a brief sketch of the origin of Islam in history. The Prophet Muhammad was born in Mecca into a prominent clan of the Quraysh. His father died before his birth, and his mother when he was very young. He then grew up in the care and protection of an extended family and in conformity with the conventions of the Quraysh. For example, he was placed in the care of a Bedouin family in order to enjoy the benefits of desert life, as well as to learn linguistic skill from the masters of the craft. As he grew older, Muhammad's reputation as a remarkable young man, well liked and respected by his townsmen, grew. He made a name for himself as a trustworthy and truthful person, to the extent of being called *al-Amīn* (the trustworthy) and *al-Ṣādiq* (the truthful). His people entrusted their valuable property with him for safekeeping.

However, their attitude towards him changed when, at the age of 40, he claimed to have undergone a religious experience. The experience turned him into a bitter foe as far as the Quraysh were concerned, but it also made him one of the most remarkable personalities in human history. Muhammad received the first revelation whilst on a vigil, in seclusion outside the town of Mecca, and soon proclaimed a new religion and way of life to the world. The people of Mecca, headed by the leading Quraysh clans, rejected his teachings and claims and resisted his attempts to preach in the city. Undeterred, he directed his attention to his family and friends, and then progressively to anybody who passed through the trading and pilgrimage centre of Mecca. Eventually, the people of Yathrib, north of Mecca and situated along a crucial caravan route, invited him to settle among them. They promised to follow the new religion and to protect the Prophet against the Quraysh. After thirteen years of harrowing insults and rebuffs in Mecca, he arrived in Yathrib, later to be called the City of the Prophet. Here, he laid down the foundation of the first Islamic community, in political, social and religious terms (see Figure 1).

The Quraysh, however, did not leave him alone, thus leading to a bitter struggle between the old order and the new religious challenge. A series of political manoeuvres and wars eventually led to the establishment of the new religious community. The Prophet transformed almost every aspect of Arab life by infusing it with the consciousness of God and moral principles. From warfare to family relations, a new religious order emerged over the old. Eventually, the new order conquered Mecca and transformed it too from a centre of polytheism into a centre of Islam and the unity of God.

The call to prayer was an important part of the early religious sense of Islam. As the above sketch portrays, the original call to prayer brought believers together for worship and symbolically formed the first community. Even today, at the end of the twentieth century, the call to prayer still represents a crucial symbolic act, establishing an Islamic presence in a village, town, city or country. Many Muslims feel that an Islamic community only really comes into being when the call to prayer can be heard in their homes. The mosque may be a physical symbol of Islam, but the call to prayer is a ritual act which sets that symbol into motion by calling people together.

This chapter will follow the symbols and issues that emanate from the narrative of the call to prayer which opened the chapter. The call to prayer turns our attention to the formation of the first Muslim community and state, becoming a symbol for the formation of all subsequent Muslim communities. As we take a closer look at the narrative, we also get a glimpse of the relationship between Islam and other religions. This provides us with an opportunity to pursue the question of religious pluralism implicit in the statement. The formation of a community immediately raises the issue of its boundaries and of exclusion. The relationships among the members of the community become clear when those who do not belong are identified. This important subject for our world at the turn of the century will constitute our first foray into the symbol of the mosque. The narrative of the call to prayer also points to the symbol of height in mosques and in Islam,

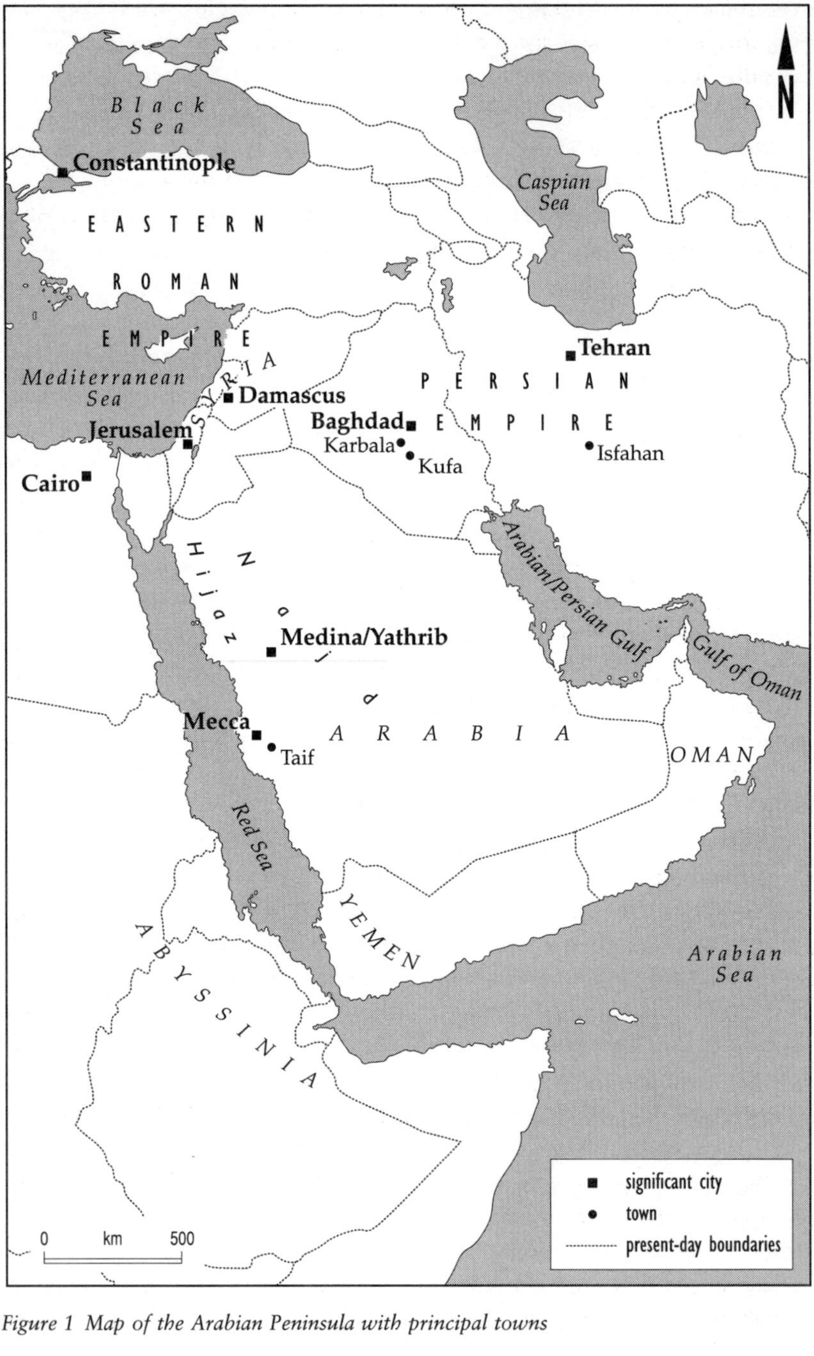

Figure 1 Map of the Arabian Peninsula with principal towns

exemplified by Bilāl finding a raised place from which to announce the time for prayer. This chapter will introduce readers to the significance of the tall minarets that grace so many city skylines. The use of the human voice in the call will be an opportunity to explore the notion of Qur'ānic recitation in Islam, as well as the ambivalent place of music in the religion. The chapter concludes with a brief note on modern amplification of the call to prayer, providing an opportunity to look at the interface between Islam and technology in the modern age.

ISLAM AND THE OTHER

At the most practical level, the call to prayer is a sign that reaches out from the mosque and beckons the believers to worship. Since its inception, however, the call has appropriated new meanings and significations, which have become as much part of Islam as the act of bringing people together and announcing the presence of a community. The narrative quoted at the beginning of the chapter makes a special attempt to set the Islamic call to prayer apart from Judaic and Christian practices. The statement is a recognition and an assertion that Islam, Judaism and Christianity were different, but also comparable. They were different in that they employed different means of calling the faithful to worship. And yet, the principle of forming a community around communal worship was a common link among the three, the difference lying only in the manner of calling. This unique relationship between Islam and these two other Abrahamic traditions echoes in theology, mysticism and many key concepts and practices in Islam. It permeates how Muslims pray, dress, and conduct statecraft. This is not surprising. As the youngest of the three monotheistic traditions, Islam has had continuously to affirm its distinctiveness from Judaism and Christianity, while at the same time appealing to the standards established by its predecessors. This balance between distinctiveness and shared heritage may be briefly explored in Islam's relations with other religions. It forms one of the cornerstones of Islam's approach to Judaism and Christianity, and potentially to other faiths as well.

The following verse in the Qur'ān appeals to the common link between the three faiths:

> Say: O people of the book! Come to common terms as between us and you: that we worship none but God; that we associate no partners with

> him; that we erect not, from among ourselves, Lords and patrons other than God.
>
> (Qur'ān 3:64)

The worship of God, and the sacred text as the foundation of the religious community, are the common grounds to which the verse appeals. Muslims have always identified and recognized the presence of a sacred book in other religious communities. In fact, this acceptance constitutes one of the articles of faith in Islam. Both aspects of religion, worship as well as a sacred book, represented a powerful inspiration for inclusivism, suggesting a starting point for at least Jews, Christians and Muslims to begin dialogue and co-operation. This does not mean that other religions are in principle excluded. Extending inclusivism even further, it represents an inspiration for Muslims to seek similar common grounds among religions in general.

However, this inclusivism is not the only Islamic attitude to other religions. In contrast to the verse quoted above, the following suggest that Islam has superseded and replaced its predecessors:

> Behold the only true religion in the sight of God is self-surrender unto Him (*islām*); and those who were given the book before took, out of mutual jealousy, to divergent views only after knowledge had come to them. As for him who denies the truth of God's messages, behold, God is swift in reckoning.
>
> (Qur'ān 3:19)

> Whoever wishes anything else but Islam, it will not be accepted.
>
> (Qur'ān 3:85)

In these verses, Islam is the criterion by which other religions are judged. Here, the distinctiveness of the Islamic tradition is stressed and its exclusive claim to truth is attested. The following verse even declares that the true religion, *dīn*, will prevail over all other religions:

> He is the one who has sent his messenger with guidance, and the religion (*dīn*) of truth, so that it prevails over all religion (*dīn*), even though the disbelievers detest it.
>
> (Qur'ān 61:9)

Islam's relation with other religions, therefore, is neither entirely exclusivist nor completely inclusivist. It accepts in principle the fact that some form of co-operation, on certain specific matters, may become a basis for mutual respect, even salvation. On the other hand, it is sufficiently exclusive to make a claim to truth and specificity.

Some modern commentators have tried resolve these different approaches in the Qur'ān. From a historical point of view, it has been argued that the different teachings in the Qur'ān should be related to the experience of the first Muslim community with Jews and Christians. The reconciliatory, even pluralistic, tone of the Qur'ānic verses reflects the good relations between Islam and its Abrahamic cousins, while the exclusivist approach reflects the political conflict with particular religious communities. Thus, at the very beginning of the Prophet's career, he expected the religious communities to accept his new message, and this is reflected in the Qur'ān's reconciliatory and positive approach to other religions. On the other hand, a hardened approach towards other religions in the Qur'ān is a reflection of intense political problems that followed later. In each case, relations between Islam and other religions are not entirely determined by theological arguments: social and political factors also apply in determining such relationships.

Contemporary scholarship has debated extensively over the dating of the Qur'ānic verses and the social and political development of the early Muslim community. There is no unanimity as to exactly when and how the Qur'ān matches the unfolding social and political history of early Islam. Thus, for example, it has been argued that the occurrence and significance of Abraham in the Qur'ān serves to transcend the Jewish and Christian claims to exclusive salvation. Such an image was employed by the Prophet and the Qur'ān in a discussion with Jews and Christians, and the Qur'ān's appropriation of Abraham challenges the Jews' and Christians' claims to possess the truth. On the other hand, others argue that the figure of Abraham had earlier been employed in the Qur'ān as the originator of the Meccan sanctuary. Hence, in spite of the sense that verses and contexts are closely intertwined, the exact dating of the Abraham image in the Qur'ān is not resolved in a direct and simplistic manner. Paret presents these competing arguments, and then captures the gist of the historicist argument for the relationship between text and context:

> Muhammad in his appropriation of the Abraham idea was not as clearly and deliberately constructive, but more generally redeveloped and appropriated well-known elements of his life in an organic manner. This

> appropriation took place in a skillful discussion with his Jewish and Christian opposition.
>
> (Paret 1991: 121)

Thus, the issue of historical location of specific verses of the Qur'ān is not quite resolved. It does not seem a simplistic relationship between text and context, nor is it a case where text and context are completely detached from each other.

This historicist approach has no doubt alarmed Muslims who regard the Qur'ān as a revelation that is not determined by historical demands. This problem is not unique to Islamic scripture, but is true of other religious communities and texts as well. The historicist approach has generally pitted religious communities against the non-confessional, historicist study of religion. In terms of the latter, truth is the effect of concrete historical realities.

In the Islamic case, however, a parallel approach to the study of the Qur'ān comes close to a historicist approach. Muslim scholars were aware of, and believed in, the gradual descent of the Qur'ān and its close connection with the historical experience of the early community. The study of the Qur'ān in exegesis recognized this relationship and developed the science (*'ilm*) of the occasions of revelation (*asbāb al-nuzūl*). In this particular field of study, Muslim exegetes tried to locate the specific occasions during which the Qur'ān was revealed. In its best form, this is a historical mapping of the text within the career of the Prophet Muhammad. As in the historicist approach, verses in the Qur'ān are related to very specific historical contexts, which scholars then use to elaborate Islamic legal and ethical teachings. Unlike the historicist approach, however, the majority of scholars make no inference about the value of the verses and the teachings as absolute truths. Different situations demand different responses, but this does not demand a reflection of truth as such. In the Islamic context, the historical nature of the verses has urged some Muslims to consider the adaptability of specific Islamic teachings. Fazlur Rahman, a modern scholar of Islam, has urged Muslims to revisit this particular discipline in order to deal with contemporary issues facing Muslims (Rahman 1982: 17). He himself has been an advocate of change in Islamic legal issues, and finds the *asbāb al-nuzūl* an ideal and authentic mechanism for dealing with it. Other scholars vaguely suggest that the historical rootedness of the text should open the door for contemporary reflection. Of course, the historicist claim goes much further than the Islamic *asbāb al-nuzūl*, by suggesting that the context determines the text, and thus the values and principles of Islam. Consequently, a meticulous historical study of the text, and its implications for Islamic ethics, remains an anathema for most Muslims.

The historical approach to the verses in the Qur'ān may be contrasted with a linguistic approach, which offers a different solution to the relationship between Muslims and other religions. In this regard, the terms *islām* and *dīn* in verses orientated towards exclusivism ought to be taken in their generic sense of 'commitment and surrender to God'. Instead of the verses establishing Islam's exclusive claim to truth, they are also the foundations for an inclusive interpretation of religions. All religions are forms of commitment and surrender (*islām*). Islam is thus not a unique and distinctive tradition, as the verse seems to imply on a first reading, but a universal relationship and attitude towards God or an ultimate authority. Focusing on the verbal character of the term *islām*, a modern commentator on the Qur'ān calls it 'self-surrender to God' (Asad 1980: 257).

A leading Muslim proponent of religious inclusivism, Hasan Askari, also proposed a poignant interpretation of *islām*, which holds major significance for understanding the diversity of religions from an Islamic perspective. His words are worthy of repetition:

> Islam, as the name of the religion Muhammad preached, was a natural outcome of both the critique and the affirmation of Judaism and Christianity. But the very concept was a two-edged sword. By the very connotation of the word, *islām* cannot be restricted to a particular historico-collective group who came to follow the *sunnah* of the Prophet.
> (Askari 1985: 198)

For Askari, *islām* was a fundamental orientation towards the Ultimate which both Muslims and others were expected to heed. Askari went even beyond inclusivism to suggest that all religions must search for the history-transcending glimpse of the Absolute. When *islām* as an orientation and attitude was adopted for a particular religion, it carried the seeds of its own self-criticism. Such a subtle reading of *islām* as an attitude and orientation is certainly plausible. It takes advantage of the tremendous potential that exists in the nuances of a word or concept. Both *islām* and *dīn* are important attitudes, and can easily be seen to refer to attitudes and forms of commitment and surrender in other religions.

They are not the jealously guarded property of Islam as a particular historical community.

It must be pointed out, however, that the argument is not entirely convincing to many Muslims. This is not merely because of their narrow-mindedness, but because the argument is a sophisticated challenge to reading the Qur'ān in a twentieth-century global context. The subtlety of the distinction between Islam as a religious tradition and *islām*, meaning commitment or surrender, cannot be completely eliminated by insightful interpretation. While both *islām* and *dīn* may be reasonably interpreted as generic attitudes and relations, the Qur'ānic verses alluding to them were also establishing particular forms of historical traditions. Both Islam as a religious tradition and *islām* – commitment, surrender and transcendence – were implied. It is clear that in the first two verses quoted above (Qur'ān 3:19 and 3:85), *islām* is contrasted with those who had already had revelations, 'those who were given the book' in the past. And in the case of *dīn* in Qur'ān 61:9, the contrast and difference between God's messenger's religion, namely Islam, and all other religions, cannot be ignored. In short, the dictionary and philosophical connotation of singular words and concepts cannot ignore the syntax of the verses in the service of an inclusivist interpretation of faith.

This position in Islam, therefore, should be seen neither as an uncomplicated inclusivism, nor as a testimony to exclusivism par excellence in world religions. The historical location of these verses in the seventh century suggests that theological positions are subject to change. Such a change was also evident within the lifetime of Muhammad. On the other hand, the linguistic interpretation of *islām* and *dīn* suggests inclusivist directions. Islam shared with others, but also differentiated and distinguished itself. The call to prayer was a fine example of the balance between inclusivity and exclusivity. It was at once a recognition of a common boundary, and a statement of distinctiveness.

Perhaps this may be a point of departure for appreciating the pluralism of traditions. Beyond exclusivism, which claims absolute truth to the exclusion of all paths to God, and inclusivism, which accepts truth only in one's own image, pluralism accepts a level of distinction and discontinuity between one tradition and another. The discontinuity does not pose a problem but an opportunity for recognition, perhaps even for competition to do good. The following verse in the Qur'ān presents such a possibility:

> For every group have we [God] made law and a way. And if God wished, he would have made you a single community, but he wants to test you with what he has given you. So compete with each other in doing good. To God is your return, all of you, when he will inform you about that which you differed with each other.
>
> (Qur'ān 6:48)

This verse, read in conjunction with those that stress the inclusivism or exclusivism of Islam, points rather to the uniqueness of a tradition. It opens the possibility of different religious communities contributing to the common good for the sake of their own salvation and relationship with God.

HEIGHT AS SYMBOL

The call to prayer suggests another important aspect of Islam. Many reports narrate how Bilāl climbed onto a high place and delivered the call to prayer so that as many people as possible could hear him. Bilāl's taking of a high place for the call to prayer symbolized all subsequent minarets, as they too rose to facilitate the call to prayer. This act of Bilāl rising resonated in the rising minarets of the grand mosques in Istanbul, Cairo and Timbuktu. It initiated an architectural style which became an inextricable aspect of mosques in most parts of the Islamic world. As a functional instrument for the amplification of the human voice, the height of a minaret was a natural and obvious symbol of the Islamic call to prayer.

The account in the foundation documents of Islam of Bilāl's climbing on top of a building directly established the value of height for Islamic buildings. The height of a minaret is a visual counterpart to the sound of the muezzin (the caller to prayer). As the call to prayer reaches out to the community, the height of the minaret stands out among the buildings of a city and town. Both sound and vision act together to present the mosque and its message to the world. Beyond these visual and auditory symbols to the society and community out there, the minarets also seem to be symbolizing that which is beyond the here and now. As the minarets rise upwards in the sky, they point to something beyond this material world. The sky to which the many minarets point has always symbolized God beyond the here and now, the source of the Ultimate and the measure of good. Certainly, this is how many Muslims regard minarets, both those of the great mosques of Islam and of the many smaller and humbler structures in towns and villages.

The question of tall minarets, however, cannot be left at this sublime level. Unfortunately, closer examination reveals that the symbolism of height and the grandeur of exquisite monuments to one God has often been used for less than spiritual reasons. As in many other religions, the power of transcendence has often been placed at the service of more mundane objectives. Closer historical study shows that height was first used by Muslim rulers to symbolize power and authority. The rulers' audience halls were the first buildings to exploit space and height as symbols of authority. Later, this was extended to the use of the tower and minaret. Historical evidence has attested that using the tall slender minaret to call the faithful to prayer was a later development in the architecture of Islam: it was first used by Muslim authorities to make a statement of power, to assert their own authority through the apparent authority of God. The Islamic dynasties that followed Muhammad and his close associates chose tall slender minarets as part of the regalia of royal dominion over the most sacred places in Islam. The first such dynasty, the Umayyads, who ruled the Islamic heartland from Damascus between 661 and 750, used height in this way. This dynasty was founded in the aftermath of a civil war within Islamic society, and represented the old Arab families who had been the staunchest opponents of the Prophet in Mecca. They had become Muslims late during the life of the Prophet Muhammad, but with the success of the new Islamic power they rose quickly through the military and administrative machinery of the early caliphate. With its origins in the intractable problems of leadership in the rapidly growing community, the Umayyad dynasty was built on the ashes of a bloody civil war. Naturally, the Umayyads were eager to search for symbols of legitimacy among Muslims, and built tall minarets over the mosque in Medina (Bloom 1989: 43–4).

Symbols alone, however, could not ensure their power and they were deposed by the Abbasids in 750, accused of gross political and religious iniquities. The new rulers claimed to be the legitimate rulers, as members of the family of the Prophet. Soon, however, they too became a family dynasty, although one claiming to be carrying a mandate from the Prophet Muhammad, and to be his descendants through the line of 'Alī, his cousin and son-in-law, as well as 'Abbās, a paternal uncle of the Prophet. From an architectural point of view, the Abbasid contribution to Islam was the building of tall minarets in Mecca to match those in Medina. In fact, al-Mahdi, the third Abbasid caliph who ruled from 775 to 785, used minarets to establish a hierarchy of religious structures. He shortened the minarets in Medina which the Umayyads had built, and made the ones in Mecca tall and slender (Bloom 1989: 53). Minarets, then, were first built as symbols of the most important places in Islam. The minaret was not part of the standard features of all mosques at the time but, as Bloom rightly suggests, 'the first significant step towards the exteriorization of a previously interiorized type, for it powerfully indicated the mosque's presence beyond its immediate boundaries' (Bloom 1989: 19). Moreover, Bloom traced the minarets to the building of towers along the pilgrimage routes which were 'not erected as convenient sights for weary travelers but as a sign of the presence and power of the ruler' (Bloom 1989: 45).

In early Islamic history the tall tower of the minaret as a feature for mosques was introduced much later in some areas outside Arabia (Bloom 1989: 57). It remained a source of controversy in the west of Islam, Morocco, as well as among minority Islamic traditions. In contrast to the regions where the central authorities held sway, fringe groups did not accept the height of the mosque as a natural development. In fact, this seems to be true even of the non-political authorities in the Islamic tradition. When we move from the perspective of the rulers to discussions among jurists, the place of minarets becomes even more dubious. A careful look at the religious literature indicates that tall and ostentatious buildings were incompatible with the Prophetic ideal of simplicity and moderation. The following statement attributed to the Prophet places a negative value on all buildings:

> Anas b. Mālik narrated that the Prophet said: Spending for yourself and your family are all regarded as spending for the sake of God, except buildings because there is nothing good in these.
>
> (Ibn al-'Arabī al-Mālikī, n.d.: IX, 298)

> Ibn Mājah narrates: The Messenger of God passed by a dome over the door of a person from Medina, and inquired: 'What is this?' They replied: 'It is a dome built by somebody.' The Messenger of God said: 'All which is like this is a calamity on its owner on the day of judgement.' The Medinese person heard this, and broke it down. When next the Prophet passed by, and did not see it, he asked about it. He was informed that the man had broken it down when he heard the Prophet's response to it. The latter then responded: May God have mercy on him; may God have mercy on him.
>
> (Ibn Mājah n.d.: II, *Book of Asceticism*, no. 4161).

From the perspective of these statements, clearly, the mosque and its tall stately minarets were an anomaly in relation to the values of asceticism and devotion to God. The height and majesty of a tower seemed completely to nullify the acts of submission and self-negation that constituted worship inside the mosque. The very word 'mosque' is derived from the Arabic *masjid*, meaning 'a place for prostration'. It was not surprising, therefore, that political rulers, not religious groups, were the first to exploit the architecture of height in a mosque. Religious acceptance of the tall tower was slow, ambivalent, and contested.

In addition to their religious significance as symbols of God's transcendence, then, minarets have also been used by the rich and powerful to make their statement in society, carrying their message from the mosques of capital cities and ordinary villages (Gilsenan 1990: 177). It certainly seems that religious symbols are readily subverted and exploited for different purposes. At the end of the twentieth century, mosques and their graceful minarets stand in stark contrast to the powerful and dominant architecture of modernism. This, however, should not create the impression that beauty and grace cannot also exude power and dominance. The minaret's rising to the skies has to be continually affirmed and defended if it is not to be subverted.

MUSIC AND THE HUMAN VOICE

We move now to yet another connotation of the Islamic call to prayer: the place and use of the human voice and music. Our narrative of the call to prayer indicates that the early Muslim community rejected musical instruments in favour of the human voice. Since then, the call to prayer has been a powerful and compelling symbol of the human voice in Islam. As it rises five times a day from mosques throughout the world, it raises the human voice above every other sound, melody or din. The human voice has become the highest and supreme symbol of the beauty of sound in Islamic culture and civilization. The call to prayer in this sense is closely associated with a number of other forms in Islamic culture. It recalls the importance of the human voice in the recitation of the Qur'ān, the authentic narration and the poignant poem in Islamic cultures. In each of these auditory forms, Islamic culture celebrates the beauty and mastery of the human voice.

The use of the human voice is most exemplary in the recitation of the Qur'ān. As the sacred text in Islam, it is not surprising that the Qur'ān has been the object of a tremendous amount of scholarship and analysis. As with any other classical text, both early and modern scholarship has left no stone unturned to explore the nuances of the word of God. This exploration took the form of the discipline of *tafsīr* (exegesis) whereby the text has been meticulously analysed. Linguistic, historical and mystical insights have been drawn from the text, thereby expanding the meaning of the Qur'ān for Muslims from one generation to the next. Muslims, however, also appreciate the Qur'ān as a beautifully recited text, not only as an object for intricate exegesis. Their association with the Qur'ān begins from childhood or from when they first embrace Islam. Muslims memorize a few short passages of the Qur'ān for prayer, including, at the very least, the opening chapter (*al-fātiḥah*) and short chapters from the end. The intimate association between believer and the Qur'ān is not restricted to a text, but is alive as a sound form. It is this association that endures through a person's life, even when Arabic is not the mother tongue of the believer or its difficult syntax is not clearly understood.

Some recent studies on the importance of recitation in Islam have focused on its ability to recreate or recall the act of revelation. As Muslims recited the word of God verbatim, they recalled the first act of revelation when the angel Gabriel appeared to Muhammad in a cave outside Mecca and ordered him to recite. Let us pick up the story from Martin Lings' very popular modern biography of the Prophet Muhammad:

> it was one night towards the end of Ramadan, in his fortieth year, when he was alone in the cave, that there came to him an Angel in the form of a man. The Angel said to him: 'Recite!' and he said: 'I am not a reciter,' whereupon, as he himself told it, 'the Angel took me and whelmed me in his embrace until he had reached the limit of mine endurance. Then he released me and said: "Recite!" I said: "I am not a reciter," and again he took me and overwhelmed me in his embrace, and again when he had reached the limit of mine endurance he release me and said: "Recite!", and again I said "I am not a reciter." Then a third time he overwhelmed me as before, then released me and said:
>
> > Recite in the name of thy Lord who created,
> > He created man from a clot of blood.
> > Recite; and thy Lord is the Most Beautiful,
> > He who hath taught by the pen,
> > taught man what he knew not.
>
> (Qur'ān 96:1–5; Lings 1983: 43)

This was the first revelation (*waḥy*) to Muhammad and they continued until his death twenty-three years later. Immediately after the demise of the Prophet, Muslim tradition believes that the Qur'ān was compiled into 114 chapters (*sūrah*) consisting of over six thousand verses. The longest chapter has 286 verses covering a variety of topics, while the shorterst chapter, on the unity of God, consists of only 3. One may recite selected portions from the Qur'ān, preferably shorter pieces in congregation and longer ones when alone.

The revelation was in the form of a recitation, and Gabriel's recitation of the Qur'ān to Muhammad became a model for all subsequent recitations. As Kristina Nelson put it so beautifully, when Muslims recite the Qur'ān, they want to capture the 'sound of the revelation as Muhammad learned it' (Nelson 1985: 7). The first recitation was the most significant recitation, enabling and facilitating subsequent inspirations in history. It became the means through which one contemplated one's responsibilities towards God. Note that this is not necessarily a cognitive exercise in which one understands the intricacies of the Arabic language. Although the latter is most desirable, the majority of Muslims understand little or no classical Arabic. This implies that the recitation of the Qur'ān has become an echo of, or, if you will, a meditation exercise upon what one generally understands or desires of the relationship between God and believer.

The recitation of the Qur'ān has become a very specific art form, which can be broadly divided between private and public expressions. *Tartīl* is a measured recitation ideal for private recitation as well as for use in daily prayers. All Muslims learn some form of this recitation in order to recite portions of the Qur'ān in their daily prayer. The focus in this style of recitation rests on the proper formation of consonants and the places of rests and elongation in the Qur'ānic text. The second style of recitation is called *mujawwad*. This style is an embellished form of recitation which was developed for public performance. The *mujawwad* style is the preserve of virtuosos with beautiful voices and breath control. Their recitation corresponds to the intricate artwork and designs of an exquisite prayer rug, the cadences and elongation of the recitation like the geometrical and botanic patterns of the carpet (see Figure 2). The *mujawwad* recitation originally took place in mosques and other public places, performed by professionally trained reciters. In recent years, it has become a global phenomenon with the staging of regional and international competitions. At first, Egyptian reciters held sway in the

Figure 2 Prayer rug

artful recitation of the Qur'ān. In particular, 'Abd al-Bāsiṭ 'Abd al-Ḥamad was one of the first internationally recognized reciters in modern times, and his style has been emulated in many Muslim communities throughout the globe. Women in South East Asia have also emerged as some of the best reciters of the Qur'ān and Iranians joined the field after the Islamic revolution of 1979.

The recitation of the Qur'ān celebrates the human voice. In the twentieth century, two issues have accentuated the role of the human voice in Islam. The first concerns the use of musical instruments, and the second relates to the use of technology to amplify the voice. The first issue emerged early in Islamic history and produced a debate which has periodically reappeared within the Muslim community. In the context of modern society, music has become a controversial subject, producing supporters and opponents. The second issue encapsulates the conflict between religion and modernity. It is a concrete example of how a religious tradition has responded to technological innovation, both to its opportunities and threats posed to traditional life. A brief discussion of each of these issues concludes this chapter.

The question of music is introduced in this section because the call to prayer and the recitation of the Qur'ān are forms of what Lamyā' al-Fārūqī has called 'tone-durational art' (al Fārūqī 1985: 44). She approaches the question of music in Islam from her definition of music as a 'meaningful organization of tones and durations'. In this regard, she places Qur'ānic recitation on one end of the spectrum and licentious and passion-arousing music on the other. Thus, she tries to differentiate between music condemned by scholars and 'music' associated with religious forms and experiences. Since the earliest period of Islamic history, some scholars have opposed the use of musical instruments in society in general, and for religious purposes in particular. They have justified this position on the basis of numerous Prophetic statements (*ḥadīth*) which condemn the use of musical instruments in no uncertain terms. A few of these statements illustrate the intensity of the condemnation, and the extremely negative connotations of musical instruments in Islamic rituals and society. Musical instruments are condemned:

1. On the authority of 'Ā'ishah (the wife of the Prophet) who said that the Messenger of God said: 'God forbids the female singer: selling her, her price and her education, and listening to her.'

2. On the authority of ʿAlī b. Abū Ṭālib, the Messenger of God said: 'If my community has fifteen characteristics, then calamity will befall them. Among these are the taking of singers and instruments. Accept as a consequence, red smell, distortion, and ignominy [in Hell-fire].'
3. According to Abū Dāwūd, on the authority of Ibn Masʿūd, the Prophet had said: 'Singing grows hypocrisy in the heart.'
4. In al-Bukhārī's widely recognized collection, Abū Mālik al-Ashʿarī said that he heard the Messenger say: 'Among my people will be those who will make permissible silk, wine, and musical instruments.'

The *ḥadīth* in Islam is a statement of what the Prophet Muhammad directly said, or did, and reported to subsequent generations through a reliable chain of narrators. It always consists of both a statement and a chain of narrators (*isnād*). Sometimes, as in the examples cited above, the long chain of narrators is omitted to focus on the import of the statements. The voice of the Prophet of God settles all matters in Islam, his decision and judgement resolving all disputes. This authority has been repeatedly affirmed in the Qur'ān through the phrase 'Obey God and obey the Messenger'. The following also places the authority of the Messenger beyond dispute: 'It is not for a Muslim man or woman to choose on a matter when God and his Messenger have given their decision' (Qur'ān 33:36).

In spite of the intensity of the statements, differences of opinion among Muslims with regard to music flourished. There is unanimity in the view that music may not be used in fundamental religious obligations. No music accompanies congregational worship or the call to prayer. However, there is disagreement about music beyond these specific settings. Generally, two approaches have challenged the condemnations and sustained alternative opinions on the matter of musical instruments. In the first case, some scholars have questioned their authenticity and attribution to the Prophet. In this regard, it is important briefly to introduce the science of *ḥadīth* criticism developed by Muslim scholars by the end of the first century of Islam.

For at least one hundred years after the demise of the Prophet Muhammad, Muslims shared his statements and deeds in a largely oral culture. Then, when a greater degree of dissension set in among the Muslims, special attention was given to the transmission of the statements from one person to the next. In particular, scholars investigated the nature of the chain of narrators, and eventually produced an elaborate system of classification. In spite of some regional variations, this discipline of *ḥadīth* criticism focused on two primary aspects of statements attributed to the Prophet. The first concerned an examination of the moral probity of the individual narrators, and their ability to reproduce reliable and accurate texts. Extensive biographical notices were collected, and the narrators were classified in terms of the key characteristics of morality and accuracy. Some were declared reliable (*thiqah*) and accurate (*ḍābiṭ*), while others were considered 'best left out' (*matrūk*) or even 'liars' (*kādhib*). Second, *ḥadīth* criticism also evaluated the chains of narrations for the quality of their connections to the Prophet Muhammad. Statements were then classified, and the best of these were designated 'attributed' (*marfū'*), meaning that an unbroken chain of narrators spanned across time and connected with the Prophet. Where the narrators of *ḥadīth*s could not be connected to each other, or to the Prophet, these were classified differently in order to alert Muslims to their respective deficiencies. Finally, on the basis of these two areas of investigation, Prophetic statements were declared authentic (*ṣaḥīḥ*), good (*ḥasan*) or weak (*ḍa'īf*). The discipline of *ḥadīth* is much more complex than this, but this introduction suffices to give a sense of the critical approaches which were developed to ascertain reliability and accuracy in the transmission of statements. The criticism did not question the validity of the Prophet Muhammad as a source of authority. On this, there was unanimity among Muslims of all religious tendencies. Moreover, most of the investigation was concentrated in each case on the chain of narrators and the probability that the Prophet had made such a statement.

One of the most outstanding collections of *ḥadīth* was compiled by Muḥammad b. Ismā'īl b. Bukhārī (d. 870), born in what is now known as Central Asia. His collection, *al-Jāmi' al-ṣaḥīḥ* (The authentic collection) or simply *Ṣaḥīḥ Bukhārī*, is recognized by the overwhelming majority of Sunni Muslims to be the most authoritative collection of religious texts after the Qur'ān. Al-Bukhārī was a man of Persian descent whose great-grandfather had become a Muslim. His father was a pious person interested in the study of *ḥadīth* who left him with a tidy estate with which to engage in the study of religion. Al-Bukhārī travelled extensively to a variety of Muslim cities to listen to and collect the statements of the Prophet from narrators. He was known to have a prodigious memory, both for the texts and their respective lists of narrators. It is said that al-Bukhārī was tested in Baghdad by ten scholars who mismatched the texts and their narrators, and then asked him whether he had the new traditions. Al-Bukhārī denied having heard them, but pointed out how the chains of narrators and texts should be restored. He was also highly respected for the exacting criteria he established for accepting *ḥadīth* for his authentic collection. His collection consists of 2,602 distinct Prophetic statements, which were chosen from thousands. Subsequent Muslim scholarship has found defects on the basis of his own criteria, but it has generally confirmed the authoritative stature of al-Bukhārī's collection (Azami 1977; Ṣiddīqī 1961).

Ibn Ḥazm (d. 1065), an eleventh-century scholar from Andalusia, subjected the *ḥadīth* condemning musical instruments to the standards of *ḥadīth* criticism, and found them wanting. He was a recognized authority on *ḥadīth* studies, even though controversial for his caustic remarks about his contemporaries. With respect to the first *ḥadīth* cited, he found that the chain contained a person called Sa'īd b. Razīn, and his brother. According to Ibn Ḥazm, the former was unknown to any *ḥadīth* scholars and so, obviously, was his brother. The second statement also contained numerous unknown narrators, as well as one who held the dubious distinction of being labelled 'better left out' (*matrūk*). The chain of authorities for the third statement also had an unspecified *shaykh* (a senior person or an authority); while the text of Bukhārī (statement 4 above) contained two narrators who were not known to have met each other. Ibn Ḥazm's conclusion was clear and unequivocal: 'There is nothing authentic in this issue; and everything in it is fabricated. If anything in this section were authentically attributed to the Prophet, we would not have hesitated to live by it.'

There have been many other scholars like Ibn Ḥazm, who did not categorically oppose the use of music by Muslims. Unlike Ibn Ḥazm, however, they have appealed to the context of the statements, and pointed out that the object of condemnation in the Prophet's statements was not music per se, but the immoral use of music. The Prophetic condemnation, taken as a whole, implied that music was usually accompanied by singing slave girls, drinking bouts and frivolity. Muḥammad al-Ghazzālī, a modern Egyptian scholar, accepts Ibn Ḥazm's critical arguments but has also suggested the contextual dimension of the statements:

> Singing is nothing but words. When they are good, singing is good; and when they are ugly, the songs are likewise. There are sinful songs performed in dark nights even in the presence of many lights. There is

> nothing in them but the shouts of brute instinct, and the hiss of unlawful desires. But there are also songs, well presented with noble meanings. Some may be compassionate, some may be religious, and others military, to which one may respond. These carry [people] with their melodies to lofty goals.
>
> (al-Ghazzālī 1989: 68–70)

Thus music by itself is not problematic. According to this perspective, the Prophet Muhammad only condemned it for its association with the frivolity of the court. Thus, music was acceptable as long as it did not interfere with the performance of religious duties and obligations. This argument clearly relates to the context in which the Prophet's statements were made, and suggests that we always look at the broader social context for guidance and Prophetic approval.

The historical context of the Prophetic statements has been investigated by modern critical scholarship with a different result. Unconcerned directly with the religious significance of Prophetic statements, modern historical scholarship has applied its suspicion to the statements themselves and questioned their purported attribution to the Prophet Muhammad. While Muslims looked at the context in order to understand the broader implication of the *ḥadīth*, such scholarship questioned whether the context was seventh-century Mecca and Medina. One of the earliest and foremost scholars espousing this view, Ignaz Goldziher, suggested that many *ḥadīth* bore the clear stamp of historical circumstances during which they were collected and classified:

> The group of *ḥadīth* in which the pious, as it were, mirror the conditions of the empire (putting into the mouth of the Prophet their opinions of practices of which they disapprove in order to invest those conditions with the appearance of events preordained by God) are closely linked with the political and social circumstances of the time and grew out of them.
>
> (Goldziher 1971: II, 121)

In this sense, *ḥadīth* were not so much a reflection of seventh-century Arabia as of Umayyad and Abbasid times. The Prophetic condemnations do not allude to the debauchery of Mecca, but to the singers, the slave-women, and the pomp and leisure of the later Muslim dynastic courts. It does seem plausible that religious scholars were projecting their ideals and their criticisms of the courtly life of the caliphs onto the Prophet. In opposition to the court, they proposed an almost ascetic lifestyle and an austere, sober ethic.

In contrast to these approaches to music by *ḥadīth* scholars and the political court, the mystics of Islam approached music from an entirely different perspective. For them, music was a source of spiritual perfection and ecstasy. They appealed to the deeply spiritual potential of music, and were often quite blunt about those who could not appreciate it. Thus, al-Hujwīrī (d. *c*. 1077) did not mince words when he said that 'anyone who says that he finds not pleasure in sounds and melodies and music is either a liar and a hypocrite or he is not in his right senses, and is outside of the category of the men and beasts' (quoted in Nelson 1985: 45). Another great Islamic scholar, Abū Ḥāmid Muḥammad al-Ghazālī (d. 1111), placed the role of music in a truly deep and spiritual framework:

> The heart of man has been so constituted by the Almighty that, like a flint, it contains a hidden fire which is invoked by music and harmony, and renders man besides himself with ecstasy. These harmonies are echoes of that higher world of beauty which we call the world of spirits, they remind man of his relationship to that world.
>
> (al-Ghazālī 1964: 73)

In general, some mystical orders in Islam found deep spiritual resonance in music and musical sounds. Rūmī, one of the foremost mystical poets, developed an elaborate repertoire of music for spiritual devotion. In contemporary times, the followers of his teachings and spiritual discipline are known by their dance and music as the Whirling Dervishes. Rūmī's exquisite poetry often used the reed-flute as a metaphor for spiritual relations and states:

> If I am full of wind, it is because I am a flute and Thou are the Flutist.
> Since Thou art my Self, Oh Beloved, I am self-satisfied.
> The lovers lament like reeds, and love is the flutist.
> What marvelous things will Love breathe into this flute of the body.
> The flute is manifest and the Flutist hidden
> In any case, my flute is drunk from the wine of His lips.
> Sometimes He caresses the flute, sometimes He bites it.
> Ah! I lament at this hand of this sweet-melodied, flute-breaking Flutist.
>
> (Quoted in Chittick 1983: 272)

Many mystical orders in Islam have developed inspirational music which is still extremely popular today. Some aspects of this tradition, like the *qawwālī* (devotional songs) of South Asia, have become world famous as musicians and musicologists map the world of music. In each of these cases, the practice of music is closely associated with the development of the soul.

Clearly, there were a number of positions within Islam with regard to music. One, represented by the *ḥadīth* statements quoted above, opposed the use of music, particularly that kind of music related to its immoral location in the political realm of the court. On the other hand, mystics saw great potential in music. The disagreement rested not only in the proofs that were adduced by each party. The *ḥadīth* scholars and mystics proposed different means to attaining nearness to God. For the scholars, music represented frivolity, as it was associated with kings, wealth and debauchery. The mystics, on the other hand, regarded music as one of the fundamental symbols of, and means towards, spiritual fulfilment and ecstasy.

The debate on music has been revived in modern times, and some of the arguments presented here have been reproduced in Muslim society. To a certain extent, these debates on music do not directly address the concerns of modern music, whether classical European music or the deluge of twentieth-century styles. Early Islamic debates revolved around the idea of music as a special, privileged preserve of the royal court or a means to spiritual development and ecstasy. Modernization has affected both domains. Music is popularized to such an extent that it is no longer constrained by the requirements of wealth and privilege. Musical forms are not constrained by long-lasting conventions, but are now determined by popular demand and market forces. Second, spiritual development hardly plays a role in any notion of human development as conceptualized by some of the mystics. In spite of these anomalies, modern Islamic scholarship continues to appeal to the historical debates to support one or other view. These debates generate occasions for pamphlets, books, and radio and television talk shows, but by their very repetitive nature they fail to address the meaning and significance of modern music. Largely a product of leisure, music in modernity plays a significant role in the homes of most Muslims; ordinary Muslims all over the world experiment with and explore modern music. The religious debates, however, lag far behind such developments.

In spite of attempts to debate the issue, the debate on music suggests the de facto secularization of Muslim society. While scholars try to create the impression that Islam addresses all aspects of life and places a value on every issue that arises, their failure to address the challenges of modernity only creates an illusion of Islamization. At the level of public discussion, it appears that such questions are adequately addressed and appropriate rulings pronounced upon them. In fact, by failing to address the questions that arise directly from modernity, such responses allow the actual practices of Muslims to escape judgement. If Islamic rulings are supposed to act as a filter for all human acts, modern music falls right through its porous gaps.

THE CALL TO PRAYER AMPLIFIED: TECHNOLOGY AND RELIGION

The call to prayer in modern contexts provides an opportunity to address the interface between Islam and modernization. Like all previous social transformations, modernization makes a significant demand on religious concepts and practices. Until the 1970s, it was generally believed that the impact of modernization would erode religion altogether. Even though this has not happened, there is no doubt that rational empiricism, science, individualism, technological innovation and its implementation, all key components of modernity, make a tremendous impact on religion and religious practices.

At the beginning of the twentieth century, Muslims in India were engaged in an intense debate on the use of technology in religious practices. When sound amplification became possible through technological means, some Muslims began using it as a means for carrying sound across a prayer congregation. In Islam, the leader (*imām*) stands in front and performs the worship, which consists of a series of recitations and movements. Those standing behind him listen to the recitations and follow his movements closely. In a large congregation, where the voice of the leader cannot be carried far enough, relays of human magnifiers (*mukabbir*) used to repeat the recitation of formulas that signal the change in movement through a cycle of worship. By repeating the crucial formulas, these individuals played a role in keeping a large congregation in step with the leader. The invention of a sound magnification system seemed ideally suited for replacing the magnifiers. Moreover, it would allow the congregation to listen not only to the formulas but also to the sermons and the full recitation of the Qur'ān. The sound amplification system would at once not only replace an old system, but 'improve' on its original intention of keep the congregation together. This is what eventually happened, but not before generating an interesting debate which illustrates the manner in which Muslims approached modern science and innovations.

The discussion here will be limited to an evaluation of juridical views (*fatwā*) published by Muftī Muḥammad Shafī', a great jurist of an Indian religious seminary, Deoband. This is an important modern institution and merits some elaboration. The Dār al-'Ulūm in Deoband was established in 1867 soon after the British had assumed complete control of India. Founded by Muḥammad Ya'qūb Nanawtawi (d. 1888) and Muḥammad Qasim Nanawtawi (d. 1877), it represents one of the first Islamic institutions established on two foundations, one modern and the other traditional. On the one hand, it continued the tradition of using the medium of Urdu, and not Persian as was the case in pre-British Islamic institutions. It exploited a range of modern innovations: mail order to collect donations; printing presses to disseminate basic opinions and teachings; and the reorganization of classes with timetables, examinations and other modern forms of systematization. On the other hand, the Deoband school became a major bulwark of traditional forms of piety and religious observance in India. It used modern innovations to promote traditional faith and practice. It opposed the cultural influence of Hindu practices and rejected what Metcalf calls the 'intercessionary religion' of India (Metcalf 1995). Steeped in Ḥanafī legal tradition, it has maintained the traditional approach to Islam in a way unparalleled in the modern world. The attitude of one of its illustrious jurists towards the loudspeaker gives some glimpse as to the reasons for its success and the dilemmas it faces in holding on tenaciously to tradition while reluctantly making some necessary concessions.

Muftī Shafī' has produced extensive juridical views on contemporary issues, and this includes the permissibility of the use of loudspeakers in mosques. This issue particularly dominates the text entitled, *The Islamic Legal Rules Concerning New Technology* (*Ālāt jadīdah ke aḥkām shar'ī*) (Shafī 1963). Muftī Shafī' begins his discussion by making a clear distinction between two kinds of activities in relation to worship. The first, which he calls 'devotional acts which were originally intended', are those acts which are intrinsically part of the religion. The second category, 'devotional acts which were not originally intended', are those which change over time, and can be regarded as the means towards fulfilling the originally intended acts of worship. Hence, pilgrimage falls in the first category, while riding a camel to Mecca belongs to the second category. This principle is a strikingly modern formulation of religion. It is an approach which favours the ends over the means, whereby modern technology and approaches could easily be adopted in pursuit of religious objectives. By itself, this should open the way for a series of modifications and changes to key forms of worship in Islam.

This, however, is not to be. Muftī Shafī' also worked from another deeply rooted premise which acted as a limiting factor to the first principle: the basic forms of Islamic worship were also determined by God, in the Qur'ān, as well as by the Prophet Muhammad's example. This means that, in many cases, the forms were regarded as ends in themselves. Riding a camel to Mecca would be regarded as a means to an end, but Muftī Shafī', like most other contemporary jurists, regards watching the crescent of the new moon to signal the change of month as an end in itself. Unlike riding a camel, watching the new moon is an act of worship. This second principle adduced by the Muftī controls the innovation in the first principle, by preserving the form of Islamic worship to a certain degree. While the first principle opens the possibility of considerable innovation, the second places a limit on the extent of change. Camels are excluded from modern Islamic society, but astronomical calculations are not in yet. In the final analysis, the distinction between means and end lies in the hands of reputed jurists.

In his approach to technological innovations, Muftī Shafī' also worked from yet a third assumption, namely that modern technological innovations were not new to Islamic jurisprudence. Accordingly, there was no fundamental difference between Aristotelian science, which Muslims had used before, and twentieth-century science. The Muslim jurists' approach towards the former in the past should guide contemporary jurists towards the latter. And, in Muftī Shafī''s view, Islamic juridical foundations should not be based on the assumption that a worshipper would require scientific expertise or instruments. Just as medieval astrolabes and astronomical tables were never regarded as necessary conditions for proper worship, so too should modern contraptions not become an intrinsic part of Islamic jurisprudence:

> the call to prayer cannot be given by simply looking at the calendar, and looking at the time. Nor can any Muslim accept that the muezzin sits in his room, and give the call to prayer while the speakers are located on the

> minarets and his voice transported to other places. Even those who least understand religion, will not let the Prophetic method of the call to prayer be lost.
>
> (Shafīʻ 1963: 37)

In reference to finding the direction of Mecca, Muftī Shafīʻ describes the 'natural' way in Islamic jurisprudence: 'the nearest mosques were taken into consideration, an estimate taken, and another mosque built. In this way, a series of mosques were founded and oriented on the basis of each other. When they got a sense of east, west, north, south, and the rising and setting of the sun, the direction was determined' (Shafīʻ 1963: 35). Certainly, this was not the only approach to science and technology, and early Muslim scientists went out of their way to use available methods to determine the direction of Mecca (see Abdali [1997] for a comprehensive discussion of the direction of the *qiblah* by early Islamic scientists). However, Islamic jurisprudence as conceptualized by Muftī Shafīʻ seems to have been concerned about the minimum requirements for a Muslim wishing to perform his devotion, and this did not include scientific technology and computation.

While the jurists were arguing about the validity of loudspeakers in India, they were becoming a feature of mosques elsewhere. At the time, developments in Saudi Arabia outstripped those in India and loudspeakers began to be used in Mecca and Medina. When this happened, Muftī Shafīʻ had no choice but to revisit the issue in greater detail. On the basis of the principles outlined above, the jurist took a slightly different position. He still maintained that the loudspeaker *ought* not to be used in any form of worship, basing this view on his perception of the perils of using it. Among such perils he cited the propensity of the technology to fail and sow confusion among the worshippers, as well as its potential use in one mosque to confuse those in another mosque at close proximity. However, since the loudspeaker was increasingly used in mosques all over the world, including Mecca and Medina, Muftī Shafīʻ had to deal with the question of whether a person's worship in such a mosque was valid. On this issue, the Muftī accepted that prayer in such a mosque was not necessarily invalid.

This careful permission granted to pray in a mosque where there was a loudspeaker exposed the inadequacy of traditional Islam's dealing with science in the late twentieth century. While this approach may have worked with pre-modern technological innovations, which were significantly less widespread and less invasive of daily life, it did not adequately take cognizance of the place of technology in the twentieth century. First, technology is mass produced, easily accessible, affecting and invading every facet of life. It cannot be ignored for too long as its advantages, together with its perils, are easily adopted in the remotest part of the globe. Thus, today, for example, timetables based on solar movement are used in almost every mosque. Against the prescription of the Muftī, worshippers meticulously follow clocks for timing prayer rather than observing the movement of the sun on the horizon. Clearly, science is changing the fundamental quality of the form of Islamic worship, and it is only a matter of time before other instruments are adopted as well. Thus, one cannot assume that technology in pre-modern times performed the same function as technology in the modern period. Those who do seem to be fighting a losing battle, since they do not completely reject technological inventions nor do they take control of the direction of technological change.

The reluctance to adopt an amplification system exposed some of the differences among Muslim groups. While some jurists view modern innovations with suspicion, others adopt them with open arms. Deoband itself used modern forms of organization in its early years. More recently, one could not think of modern Islamic revival without the mass circulated audio and videocassette tapes in the Middle East, enabling preachers to send their messages onto the streets of Cairo and Tehran. Mass transport has also transformed the nature of the annual pilgrimage to Mecca. Amidst this transformation, jurists such as Muftī Shafī' have tried desperately to preserve the form of Islamic worship. Taking the teachings of the Qur'ān and the example of the Prophet literally, they sometimes manage to convey the simplicity and austerity of Islamic worship. It is a battle, however, that is being lost as the adoption of technological innovations whittles away at the older forms, transforming religious practices. Today, the microphone has become an accepted part of worship. Almost all mosques have some form of amplification where once, at least in India, it was considered questionable. It seems that Muslims do eventually adopt the technology, after an initial delay. In his analysis of new technology, Mufti Shafī' introduced a principle which distinguished between worship as such and the means of expressing it. He himself did not follow that principle, nor have many other scholars since then.

If we appreciate the devotion with which some Muslims hold on to the forms of religion in the modern world, we can also appreciate the transformation of the meaning of the respective symbol. It turns out that preserving the forms of religious practices does not preclude their transformation in modernity. When practices are held so tenaciously, their meanings are subject to change even if the forms remain the same. Religious symbols that performed a function in pre-modern society may become symbols for some other feature of the religious communities. As an example, one may think of the audible sound in the call to prayer as a signal calling people to pray. This would be its 'original' purpose and intention, as spelt out in this chapter. However, when the call to prayer becomes a point of contention with the introduction of technology, it may take on a new meaning and significance. Since technology is able to perform the original function, the religious symbol now becomes amenable to new appropriation, and the result is a proliferation of new meanings. An example from Durban, South Africa, sheds some light on the fertility of this dimension of religious life. Some citizens complained to the traffic department of the loudness of the call to prayer, upon which one group of religious scholars in the city advised the mosques to tone down the early morning call to prayer. Another group, however, regarded it as their fundamental right as citizens to call worshippers to prayer. The call to prayer, relayed by a powerful amplification system, became a fundamental symbol of Muslim presence. Any attempt to curb a once dubious contraption was immediately suspect as an intrusion on religious freedom. In such a manner, a new meaning was grafted on to the call to prayer. The great Muftī had been concerned about the amplifier's disturbance to other worshippers. In Durban, the sound of the human voice in a prayer sequence, dislodged by modern technology, was free to be exploited by social actors in their social and political claims.

This chapter has explored the symbolic connotations of the call to prayer, providing an opportunity to explore Islam's relations with other religions and belief-systems. In addition, some of the political and religious connotations of height and architectural design were brought into relief, by considering the function and meaning of the minaret. An examination of music as a sound-art and the controversy surrounding it placed the importance of the Prophet and his statements in perspective. The chapter concluded with an examination of the interface between technology and religious practices, providing an opportunity to look at a concrete example of how technology acted in the relationship between Islam and modernity.

2 ABLUTION

Purification, self-mastery and the body

Believers, when you get ready for prayer, then wash your faces and arms to your elbows, wipe your heads, and your feet up to your ankles. If you are impure from sexual defilement, then purify yourselves. And if you are ill or on a journey, and have gone to the privy or touched women, but cannot find water, then turn to pure sand and wipe your faces and arms therewith. God does not want to place a burden on you; but God wants to purify you and complete his favour upon you so that you may be grateful.

(Qur'ān 5:6)

It is narrated that the Messenger of God has said: 'When a servant performs ablution and gargles his mouth, sins fall out from his mouth; when he sprinkles water into his nose, sins fall from his nose; when he washes his face, sins fall from his face until they fall from under his eyelashes; when he washes his arms, sins fall from his arms including right under his nails; when he wipes his head, sins fall from his head until they come out from his ears; when he washes his feet, sins fall from his feet until the inside of his toenails. Then, his walking to the mosque, and his prayer is extra.'

(Narrated by Mālik and others, quoted by Sābiq 1980: I, 37)

In conformity with this Qur'ānic injunction and the Prophetic promise of ritual purification, mosques throughout the world incorporate some form of water system in their architecture. Sometimes this means that a mosque is built near a stream or a well. Classical mosques would be adorned with exquisite pools and fountains and one had to pass through water-based fixtures in order to get inside the mosque. More recently, hot and cold water mixers, stacks of individual towels and wall-to-wall tiling constitute important facets of mosque apparatus. Traditional or modern, the ritual of ablution plays an important role in determining one aspect of mosque architecture and, as we shall see, implies a notion of being Muslim.

In the last chapter, the minaret focused our attention on towers, sounds and the relations between Islam and the other. In this chapter, the ablution facilities take us one important step inside the mosque and further into Islam. In this chapter, we turn to the basic sense of purity in Islam, symbolized but not exhausted by the ritual of ablution. This means that we can explore the system that governs the rules of purity, which will take us into the larger framework of jurisprudence in Islam. Furthermore, following the meaning and acts of purity, the chapter will explore some of the significance of ritual, body and community in Islam.

PURIFICATION RITUALS IN ISLAM

A brief survey of the significance of purification and defilement is necessary in order to appreciate purification rituals in Islam. A distinction is made in Islam between real (*ḥaqīqī*) impurities and conceptual (*ḥukmī*) impurity. Real impurities include faeces, urine, blood, semen, and alcohol. These are material impurities which relate to the defilement of objects or persons. In these cases, purity is achieved by completely removing the defiling object by washing, rubbing, drying or exposure to the sun. However, some scholars have also identified conceptual (*ḥukmī*) impurity, in which there is no apparent dirt. Conceptual impurity relates to states or conditions in which humans find themselves, without necessarily being defiled by real impurities. The word *ḥukmī* refers to *ḥukm*, a command or law that determines a religious act in Islam. Consequently, we may think of *ḥukmī* impurity as a subjective determination that is related to a belief and value system. A few examples will clarify this point further. Conceptual impurity arises in the following circumstances: answering the call of nature (not actual defilement as such), touching a corpse, disbelief, menstruation and post-natal bleeding, contact with the saliva of a dog, or touching any bodily parts of the pig. Note that blood itself is a real impurity, and should be distinguished from acts like menstruation in which a person is involved as actor and agent. If a generalization is to be ventured, *ḥukmī* impurity is related to categories of thought and bodily actions, and enters the domain of worldviews and systems. In addition to the physical removal of impurities, then, such acts demand the enactment of special ritual acts that symbolically purify a person. Shāh Walī Allah (d. 1762) proposed a rationale for these impurities by suggesting that they arise in one way or another by virtue of human consumption (eating, drinking and sex). Such acts, according to Shāh Walī Allah, belong to the preserve of the lower soul which 'distracted [the higher soul] by superfluous things', and thus demand a symbolic purification (Hermansen 1996: 215).

Keeping in mind the two kinds of impurities proposed by jurists, we can now go through the major purification rituals in Islam: bathing (*ghusl*), ablution (*wuḍū'*), and *tayammum* (dry ablution) for exceptional circumstances. The first two must be performed with water that is clean, colourless, odourless and has not been used for a previous ritual. The *ghusl* is a major ritual that becomes necessary under the following circumstances: conversion to Islam, sexual relations, ejaculation, and for women, at the end of the menstrual period and post-natal bleeding. According to the Shi'ites, the *ghusl* also became obligatory after having washed a human corpse. Both Sunnis and Shi'ites recommend *ghusl* for numerous other occasions like Fridays, on the days of the two Muslim festivals (*'Īd*), for the pilgrimage, and upon entering Mecca. However, such rituals are not obligatory, and they are not necessarily intended to remove impurities. They do, of course, play an important role in the social rhythm of Islamic life.

Like other acts of worship in Islam, the *ghusl* must be preceded by an intention to purify oneself. A general washing of the entire body then follows. Even though this would technically suffice for a *ghusl*, the following more elaborate procedure and order is recommended: (1) washing hands; (2) washing the sexual organs; (3) performing the *wuḍū'*; (4) rubbing water into the roots of the hair; and (5) pouring water over the entire body, beginning from the right and going over to the left. The washing of a corpse follows a similar procedure and must be performed by at least one person in the community.

There are other forms of 'defilement' which reduce the conceptual purity of a person only to a limited degree. These are answering the call of nature, flatus, touching a person of the opposite sex (among some Sunnis), irregular bleeding (of a woman), and sleeping while resting against an object. In such a case, a bath (*ghusl*) would not be obligatory. Instead, only the minor form of purification, *wuḍū'*, would be necessary to restore purity. The essentials of the ritual of *wuḍū'* are given in the opening verse quoted at the head of this chapter: washing of one's face;

washing both arms up to the elbows; wiping part of one's head and the washing of both feet (Qur'ān 5:6). In a slightly different interpretation of the Qur'ānic verse, Shi'ites insist that feet should also be wiped, and not washed. Like *ghusl*, the *wuḍū'* also has a more elaborate procedure drawn from Prophetic recommendations. After an explicit intention, the *wuḍū'* begins with the washing of the hands, followed by rinsing of the mouth, brushing the teeth with a tooth-stick and clearing the nostrils. The face is then washed, followed by the arms (first the right and then the left). The wiping of the head comes next, followed by wiping the ears and neck in one elegant motion. The final step consist of the washing (or wiping) of the feet up to the ankles. The *wuḍū'* is best concluded with the pious invocation: 'O God! Place me among the repenters and place me among the pure.'

In exceptional circumstances, a person may be unable to maintain the condition of purity for a sufficient time to fulfil his or her obligation to pray or perform another religious duty. Such a person is called *ma'dhūr* (excused) and he or she may fulfil the duties of worship as long as the *wuḍū'* is performed on every occasion. An example of this would be a woman who bleeds irregularly. When a person is ill and cannot use water, or when water is not available in the immediate vicinity, the ritual of *tayammum* (dry ablution) may be substituted for both the *ghusl* and/or the *wuḍū'*. This ritual is performed in the following manner: (1) making an intention to purify oneself; (2) placing one's hands on clean dust and then blowing off small stones; (3) wiping face with hands; (4) repeating step two and wiping the right and then left arms up to the elbow.

A Muslim ought to maintain minimal ritual purity with a *ghusl*. Whenever any of the conditions exist that necessitate a *ghusl*, such must be performed immediately. As a form of motivation and warning, a *ḥadīth* reports that angels do not enter a home in which there is a person who requires a bath after sexual relations. The burden of allowing the flow of God's blessing to be continuous rests on all adult persons in the home. The *ghusl* is a precondition for all forms of worship in Islam. For example, a mosque may be entered by a person without the *wuḍū'* level of purity but not without the *ghusl* level of purity. Thus, according to most Sunni schools, women who are menstruating, and who therefore require *ghusl*, may not even pass through a mosque. Some Shi'ites restrict this prohibition only to the great mosques in Mecca and Medina (Khomeini 1985: 32). Similarly, menstruation and post-natal bleeding preclude women from fasting in Ramadan. When the period of menstruation is over, then a *ghusl* must be performed before religious duties are resumed. There is a difference of opinion regarding whether women may recite the Qur'ān without touching it (Jamiat ul Ulema 1981: 73).

The *ghusl* is the most general requirement for purity in terms of performing worship. This state of purity, however, consists of two levels. First, it may happen that one's purity is broken and one requires a bath (*ghusl*). Some of the conditions of this have been outlined above. Second, certain forms of defilement are not as severe, and may only require one to perform the *wuḍū'*. The first level of impurity requires only a *ghusl* but the second may be restored with *wuḍū'* only. When this is looked at from the perspective of someone preparing to worship, then it is clear that the state of purity also consists of two levels. Hence, intense religious acts like touching the Qur'ān (including the empty spaces on a page), fulfilling the obligatory prayer and circumambulating in the Meccan sanctuary (*ṭawāf*) must be performed in a complete state of purity. The *wuḍū'*, in short, is a precondition for intimate worship. Muslims perform this act regularly before the above-mentioned forms of worship. Great Muslim figures are often said to perform the night and morning prayer with one *wuḍū'*, a statement suggesting a night spent in vigil and contemplation. On the other hand, even if one is not preparing to perform a particular religious ritual, it is still required that one is not in such a state as to require *ghusl*.

The rules of purification are particularly important for worship in a mosque, but they extend beyond the mosque in the conception of the self and society. This detailed elaboration of the rituals has been necessary to provide a broad map of how ritual and rituals are constructed in Islam. So far, I have suggested that Islamic notions of purity make provision for levels of purity and also suggest a difference between real and conceptual purity/impurities. Such important considerations of purity must now be more fully explored in order to highlight how the body, the self and society emerge in the Islamic context.

THE SIGNIFICANCE OF PURITY: ISLAMIC JURISPRUDENCE

The framework for purity in Islam can be examined from a number of perspectives. In the first instance, purification should be located in the context of Islamic jurisprudence, of which it forms an important and vital part. Islam has a comprehensive code of behaviour, called *Sharīʿah*, which guides Muslim practice. The word '*sharīʿah*' literally means 'a path leading to water', and signifies a code of conduct which leads to one's salvation and felicity. God in the Qur'ān declares that this code was divinely revealed: 'For every nation, we have prescribed a path (*shirʿah*) and a method (*minhāj*)' (Qur'ān 5:48). The concept of the *Sharīʿah* implies the notion that Muslims were called by God to act in a prescribed manner. All human acts carried a value which Muslims had to identify and locate. Thus, Muslims had to seek what God desired of them in each and every situation. The rules of purity were a good example of such values. They underscored the sense of individual and social obligation and orientation in relation to self, society and God.

The *Sharīʿah* represents an ideal and a broad conceptualization of religious life in Islam. The verses in the Qur'ān and the example of the Prophet Muhammad during his lifetime elaborated this ideal. These do not, however, represent everything that Muslims regard as normative and religiously binding. After the demise of Muhammad, Muslims undertook the elaboration of this religious obligation in a systematic manner. New issues arose in public and private life, and new challenges faced the young religion as it came out of Arabia. Sometimes, they were issues in the system of government, like the administration of justice. At other times, it was a question of the public performance of religion, like the Friday prayer. Many times, as elaborated in the purification rituals given above, these issues also dealt with private matters like personal hygiene. The *Sharīʿah* as a rule of personal conduct covered both public and private practices. Over the course of two centuries, scholars constructed in each of these areas a comprehensive jurisprudence called *fiqh* (literally, understanding). This included the detailed rules in the Qur'ān and the earliest recollection of the life of the Prophet, but it was also the product of their judicial reasoning.

Fiqh consists of a body of considered opinions, arrived at by competent and prominent scholars, on what Muslims ought to be doing in their obligation to God, to other human beings, and to nature. In addition to the basic rules, scholars also debated and then more or less agreed on a systematic methodology for developing new rules and expanding the *fiqh*. Such a discipline came to be called *uṣūl al-fiqh*. If *Sharīʿah* represented the general conceptualization of individual and social obligation towards God, *fiqh* consisted of the detailed guidelines, and *uṣūl al-fiqh* (the foundations of *fiqh*) the systematic method of its elaboration.

As expected, the elaboration of the *Sharī'ah* was initially conducted in the earliest settlements of early Islam (see Figure 1). Developed by the earliest caliphs and then by an emerging class of jurists, the *Sharī'ah* took into consideration new circumstances that arose as Islamic political power expanded and the religion came into contact with different cultural traditions. The following example from Muḥammad al-Shaybānī (d. 806) illustrates the kind of questions being posed by the new circumstances. It concerns the question of what an individual soldier may take from the territory of a defeated enemy:

> It has been related from Abū al-Dardā' (a companion of the Prophet Muhammad) that he said that there is no harm if Muslim soldiers take food, bring it back to their family, eat it and also make presents of it to others, provided that they do not sell it. Now, Abū al-Dardā' seems to have included making food presents among the necessities like eating (for the soldiers themselves are allowed to eat the food in order to keep themselves alive which is a necessity). But we do not accept this for whereas eating is a basic necessity . . . making food-presents is not.
>
> (Quoted in Rahman 1965: 17)

The quotation clearly indicates the desire to develop some principles as well as a sense of obligation to perform acts. The jurist was obviously grappling with ethical considerations of what was permissible on the battlefield, as well as some general principle such as the limits imposed by necessity. As the Islamic armies became successful, they struggled with moral responsibility in difficult contexts, and the elaboration of such rules represents the code of conduct closely associated with being Muslim.

As the body of elaborate juridical rules expanded, it also reflected regional influences, as well as their political implications. The scholars were not directly engaged in politics, but their moral and ethical opinions had an important bearing on political conduct. Thus, during the second century of Islam, the scholars of Kufa, Syria and Medina each developed different schools of jurisprudence (*madhhab*, plural *madhāhib*), including both a body of expanded rulings (*fiqh*) and recognizably distinctive methods of legal reasoning (*uṣūl al-fiqh*). Thus all agreed on the Qur'ān and the Prophet as the primary sources of values, but disagreed on the secondary sources. In such matters, the Medina school was known for championing the way of the city of the Prophet; Kufa developed systematic analogical reasoning; while Syrian views were closely related to the position of the Umayyad state. Towards the end of Umayyad power, moreover, the legal schools also became part of an ideological critique of the state. The development of the schools' ethical and religious framework took on a clearly critical and independent dimension when Umayyad practices fell far short of their proposed ideals. Later, these attempts were formally brought together into a comprehensive system by Muḥammad b. Idrīs al-Shāfiʿī (d. 820).

Before we consider this great contribution to Islamic legal thought, we turn briefly to one of the earliest proponents of Islamic legal thought, al-Nuʿmān b. Thābit (d. 767) better known as Abū Ḥanīfah. His grandfather was a slave brought from Kabul to Kufa, where he was freed by a person from the Taymī Arab clan. Abū Ḥanīfah himself lived as a manufacturer and merchant of silk. He spent considerable time studying Islamic thought but refused appointment as a judge in the Umayyad establishment. Rather, he taught a group of scholars and developed his jurisprudence outside the context of a functioning legal system tied to the state. He died in prison in Baghdad and there is some difference of opinion about his imprisonment. Some say that his refusal to be appointed a judge landed him in this unfortunate position. On the other hand, according to Khaṭīb al-Baghdādī, a historian of Baghdad, Abū Ḥanīfah had made some unguarded remarks about a Shi'ite rebellion, which were interpreted as supportive of it. This is interesting, since in many other respects Abū Ḥanīfah was known to have held the view that it was not permissible to revolt against unjust rulers. Whatever the case may be, it is clear from this brief comment that Abū Ḥanīfah's remark must be placed in the context of his intellectual activity, which established an intellectual and ethical authority against political power. Abū Ḥanīfah became the reputed founder of the Kufan legal school, which was much maligned by some later schools for not strictly adhering to Prophetic *ḥadīth*. His school is supposed to have developed *raʿy* (individual opinion) as an important aspect of juridical reasoning. This became unacceptable from the point of view of al-Shāfiʿī's legal reasoning, which argued for a greatly limited scope for independent reason. Al-Shāfiʿī feared the proliferation of conflicting views in the body of Islamic legal thought. Nevertheless, the Ḥanafīs became a leading school of jurisprudence, which today enjoys wide prominence in Turkey and in the Indian subcontinent.

Al-Shāfi'ī was born an Arab Hashemite, the clan of the Prophet Muhammad, in Syria. It is said that his mother may even have been a descendent of 'Ali and Fāṭimah, and thus a Shi'ite in genealogical terms. He later pursued legal studies in Medina with Mālik b. Anas (d. 795) who was arguing for the eminence of the Prophet's city in legal decision-making and who became the founder of the Mālikī school of law. Al-Shāfi'ī was appointed to a post in Yemen, where he secretly paid homage to a Zaydi Imam, a branch of the Shi'ites opposing the central authority of the Abbasid caliphate. The plot failed, and al-Shāfi'ī was brought in chains to Baghdad. He was fortunately recognized by a jurist in the city, a student of Abū Ḥanīfah, who used his connection with the caliph to secure al-Shāfi'ī's release. After staying for a while in Baghdad al-Shāfi'ī proceeded to Egypt, where he developed his unique legal framework under the protection of one of the governor's sons. He often travelled between Medina and Egypt, but never returned to Baghdad. He died in Egypt in 820 and his grave later became a site of pilgrimage when a tomb and dome were built over it.

Shāfi'ī's systematization of Islamic legal theory was to have a deep effect on all Islamic legal schools. Al-Shāfi'ī's approach to *fiqh* brought together the key contributions from early jurists, but not without some very vehement criticisms of what al-Shāfi'ī felt were their failings and inconsistencies. Under his systematic formulation, the Qur'ān and the example of the Prophet, represented by *ḥadīth* statements, were regarded as the absolute and unassailable primary sources of law. He championed the *ḥadīth* statement as the repository par excellence of the model behaviour of the Prophet (the *sunnah*). Previously, the Mālikīs in Medina had argued that the practice of Medina should be taken into consideration in legal decisions, and the Kufans had proposed a combination of legal reasoning and history for conceptualizing the example of the Prophet. Thus, for example, Abū Yūsuf, the student of Abū Ḥanīfah, comments on a Syrian use of *sunnah*, and reveals the fluid nature of normative Prophetic behaviour in early Islam:

> Judgment regarding what is lawful and what is unlawful cannot be based upon such statements as 'People have always been practising such and such.' For, much of what people have always been practising is unlawful and should not be practised . . . the basis of judgment should be the *sunnah* of the Prophet, or of the early generations (*salaf*), i.e. the companions of the Prophet and men who have an understanding of the law.
>
> (Quoted in Rahman 1965: 30)

This statement is moving in the direction of some form of systematic legal thinking. At the same time, it does not insist that a statement attributed to the Prophet should be the exclusive source of law. Similarly, criticizing the Medinese, Abū Yūsuf writes:

> The lawyers of the Hijāz (Eastern part of Arabia including Mecca and Medina) give a decision and when they are asked for the authority they reply, 'This is the established Sunnah.' In all probability, this *sunnah* is some decision given by a market tax collector or a tax-collector in an outlying district.
>
> (Quoted in Rahman 1965: 30)

These statements reveal the different ways in which *sunnah*, the normative model for individuals and society, was envisaged in early Muslim society. For some it was the determination of political authorities, for others the customs of a city. For al-Shāfi'ī, such approaches were too imprecise and open to multiple rulings in the different regions of Islam. In place of the fluidity of *sunnah* evident in the preceding examples, al-Shāfi'ī took Abū Yūsuf's suggestion even further. Whereas the latter included the *sunnah* of the 'earlier generations . . . and men who have an understanding of the law', al-Shāfi'ī argued that *sunnah* should only be derived from *ḥadīth* statements. The latter were now thought of as the categorical imperatives which contained the normative example of the Prophet, and which ought to be used as a source of law. Only when a *ḥadīth* did not reveal a clear and unambiguous judgement was al-Shāfi'ī prepared to accept other methods of reasoning developed by his predecessors. In this regard, the Qur'ān and the Prophetic *sunnah* were the first two primary sources of law. They were followed by the consensus (*ijmā'*) of the Muslims but, more practically, of jurists and the 'earlier generations'. *Ijmā'* was the third source of jurisprudence. This was followed by a careful and conservative use of analogical reasoning (*qiyās*) whereby new rulings were founded on the basis of clearly identifiable judgements in the Qur'ān and in the *sunnah*. A Muslim jurist exercised himself to investigate these sources or foundations in order to elaborate Islamic jurisprudence. The entire process of searching for values in the sources, weighing them carefully, and arriving at a new ruling, was called *ijtihād* (exertion). This was al-Shāfi'ī's elegant and precise method of developing and discovering Islamic law. Based on the Qur'ān and *sunnah* understood in their literal import, it injected a uniformity and formality which Islamic law did not previously have.

The method of purification rituals forms an important part of this jurisprudence. Just as the ablution facilities were found at the entrance to the mosque, the book of purity (*kitāb al-ṭahārah*) constituted the first volume in many a work of Islamic jurisprudence and *ḥadīth* collection. In it, the principles and requirements of ritual purification were clearly spelt out. It included references to the Qur'ān, examples from the life and teachings of the Prophet Muhammad and the elaborations of jurists. From a jurisprudential point of view, the significance of purification lay in its divine and Prophetic location. The form and meaning of ablution was determined by the fact that God had decreed it, and that the Prophet had illustrated it in his *sunnah*. The practice of ablution was guided by a deep religious mood whereby the performer believed him- or herself to be emulating the example of the Prophet, and followed the guidelines established by the scholars.

Many observers have remarked that the *sunnah* as systematized by al-Shāfi'ī provided the uniformity of Islamic practice he had hoped for. The example of the Prophet provided a powerful, emphatic and conspicuous model of a way of life, called a paradigm-tracing model of piety by Hodgson: 'when ultimacy is sought in enduring cosmic patterns, in recurrent nature (including social nature) . . . for instance, as the worshipper faces Mecca in the mosque and bows, he sets himself symbolically in the right relation to God' (Hodgson 1974: I, 363). This eloquent statement of Islamic ritual orientation leads us to consider several implications of purity in Islam.

The first point that arises out of this particular religious focus of purity rituals is the relationship between purity rituals and purity itself. Since the overwhelming emphasis of the ritual lay in the religious value of following the literal example of the Prophet, it seems that actual purification and purity were not directly related to purity rituals. After al-Shāfi'ī, the object of purification rituals, it seems, lay in emulating a formal religious example as much as in the removal of impurities or defilement. If religious rituals in Islam had only to consider the removal of impurities, they would be open to greater fluidity in the variety of experiences of Muslims in different times and different places. This is precisely something that al-Shāfi'ī wanted to eliminate. Only the formalistic solution of the emulation of the example of the Prophet Muhammad guaranteed uniformity. In a study of the Islamic legal texts on purity, and a comparison with comparative religious phenomena, Reinhart found the Islamic ritual system unique:

> we do not find states transformed by ritual but, rather, one act requires a ritual re-action, as only the formal rather than the ontic notion of purity was of interest to the legist. It is characteristic of Islamic thought that ontology is marginal to the formal.
>
> (Reinhart 1990: 23)

Reinhart made this statement with regard to Islamic legal texts which, coming under the influence of al-Shāfi'ī's systematic framework, were bound to seek the formal rather than the ontological. In order to make this statement, the author reminded us that ritual impurity in Islam is different from purity and impurity in other religious traditions. Thus, for example, the impurity of a person under Islamic conceptualization does not render such a person impure in a deep ontological sense. Such a person does not transfer his or her impurity through contact. Thus, while menstruation was considered impure, Islamic jurisprudence did not render physical contact with a menstruating woman dangerous or defiling. Reinhart also referred to the practice of *tayammum* whereby, under certain circumstances, fine sand could be used as a substitute for water, and produce the same level of purity. For Reinhart, it was clear that Islamic rituals of purity were more than a cleansing mechanism. Under the influence of al-Shāfi'ī, they became a formal discipline.

We can pursue the meaning of this discipline by turning to anthropological insights into the symbolic dimensions of purity. These point to the creative and constructive dimension of rituals and symbols, whether derived from Islamic legal texts or from actual practices. If the Shāfi'ī approach to Islamic legal theory establishes the framework for deriving law, anthropological insights explore its particular implementation in context. The practice of rituals leads to the mapping of a cosmology for the self and society. Thus, for example, Islamic purification rituals work on the level of human relations. Notions of purification make possible or impossible certain human relations by setting off markers for interaction. Sexual relations between husband and wife, for example, are conditional upon a certain degree of ritual purity. Menstruating women are ritually impure during their normal terms of bleeding, during which sexual relations are not permitted. Some have even suggested that the touch of a menstruating woman requires that one perform the *wuḍū'* before proceeding to worship.

Similarly, some Muslims have considered disbelievers to be impure. Ayatollah Khomeini, for example, considered non-Muslims to be spiritually impure to the extent that bodily contact necessitated a ritual bath (Khomeini 1985: 20). Sunnis also consider non-Muslims to be spiritually impure, a view derived from the verse in the Qur'ān which states that 'polytheists are impure' (9:28). Sunnis, however, do not extend this notion to the requirement of a ritual for purification. In short, then, the encounter with God and encounters with other humans prescribe the scope and meaning of purity and purification.

PURITY AS COSMOLOGY

A prominent anthropologist, Mary Douglas, regards notions of purity and impurity as underscoring the cosmological systems of a people: 'ideas about separating, purifying, demarcating and punishing transgressions have as their main function to impose system on an inherently untidy experience' (Douglas 1970: 4). Symbolic structures in religion provide an opportunity for philosophizing: 'reflection on dirt involves reflection on the relation of order to disorder, being to non-being, form to formlessness, life to death' (Douglas 1970: 5). For Douglas, dirt is 'matter out of place' and has to be studied from the point of view of order in the cosmological system. Dirt and pollution provided insights on purity and order in the system.

Reinhart took this notion of symbolic purity and applied it to the Islamic norms. However, instead of the classification of order and chaos found in other traditions, Reinhart suggests that the rituals of purity in Islam exemplify moral control and discipline: 'Islamic ritual in many respects echoes the Qur'ānic summons to self-mastery' (Reinhart 1990: 19). Whenever humans release defiling substances, roar with laughter, sleep a deep sleep, and the like, they exhibit loss of control, which needed to be restored through a purification ritual, and the body 'rededicated . . . to obedience of the will' (Reinhart 1990: 16). Thus, rituals of purity are more than the process of identifying dirt and removing it. They are part of the significance of being and becoming human in relation to ultimate reality. This insight can be explored in relation to the performance of *ghusl* and *wuḍū'* as discussed above. A person remains in a constant state of purity as long as it is not nullified by any real or conceptual impurity. When defilement occurs, the legal and social system demands a restoration.

Reinhart was correct in his assessment of Islamic purification rituals as far as the legal texts were concerned. However, the problem lay in his identification of Islamic legal texts with Islam as such. Such texts have no doubt had a profound influence on Islamic thought and practice, but they do not completely determine Islam in an eternal, essentialist manner. In spite of the profound influence of al-Shāfiʿī on Islamic legal thought, we should anticipate some variation in Islamic understanding towards purity and purification. As I have argued, the formalization of the legal system was a gradual process, and we should expect to see the remnants of the early notions of purity in Islamic practices. This Qur'ānic sense of purity, if I may so call it, can be contrasted with the legalistic sense of purity rituals as outlined in the formulaic system of *Sharīʿah*. The Qur'ān refers to purity, purification and impurities in a non-ritualistic sense and thus in a non-formal manner:

> God loves those who repent, and those who are pure.
>
> (Qur'ān 2:222)

> And your garments purify them.
>
> (Qur'ān 74:4)

> Turn to pure sand and wipe your faces and arms therewith.
>
> (Qur'ān 5:6)

There is a deeper spiritual resonance in these verses, to which I shall return later in this chapter, but they do not only refer to the purification process as a symbolically repeated event. Rather, their focus lies on cleansing and purification as moral acts that apply to actual physical properties. The justification for *tayammum* in the Qur'ān, for example, is not as Reinhart suggests, an indication that purification in Islam is non-ontological. The use of sand is clearly both an exception and a concession: 'If you do not find water, then turn to pure sand . . . God does not want to place a burden upon you, but God wants to purify you, and complete his favour upon you, so that you may show gratitude' (Qur'ān 5:6). The reference, therefore, is to purification as a moral and ethical imperative in spite of the absence of water. However, by itself, it does not mean that physical aspect of purification is unimportant. This may be true of Islamic legal texts as they elaborate the rules of purification on the basis of founding documents like the Qur'ān and the *sunnah*. It is not true of these founding documents themselves. In these, there is an engagement between the physical, moral and religious which is lost in the legal structure. Perhaps, as we move away in time from the origin of a foundation text, the symbols keep us engaged. But they do so at the expense of our engagement with the world.

LIFE CYCLE AND RITES OF PASSAGE

I have pursued the significance of purity in terms of Islamic legal foundations, and then turned to its possible meaning for a Muslim's orientation to the world. Purification rituals play an important role in identifying borders and they expose the fundamental orientation of a culture's worldview. These rituals also play an important role in the life cycle of an individual. Since they are often required or mandatory during rites of passage, we now explore the important turning points in an individual Muslim life. I will explore here the meaning of birth, puberty, marriage and death, all of which provide a sense of growing up in a Muslim home.

Birth is a joyous event in any home, and this is equally true of a Muslim home. Reflecting on the norm of pre-Islamic Arabia, the father of a girl-child who frowns is severely chastised in the Qur'ān: 'When one is given the glad tidings of a girl-child, his face turns dark and he becomes angry. He hides from the people the bad omen which greets him. Shall he hold [the new-born] lightly or shove it in the sand? How evil do they reckon?' (16:59). Girl or boy, the birth of a child should always be a sign of the grace and bounty of God. It is a time for celebration and a time for thanking God and the Qur'ān takes pains to insist that there should be no gender discrimination in this regard. Unforunately, though, this rule is flagrantly violated in numerous Muslim communities.

Ritually speaking, it is the responsibility of the parents to declare the call to prayer into the ears of the infant immediately after birth. At the same time, a miniscule piece of sweet date or something similar will be placed in her mouth. And then, on the seventh day following birth, the child must be given a good name, all her hair removed and an animal sacrificed. In some places, the birth ceremony on day seven can become an elaborate event when the child is officially given a name and admitted into the community of believers. A good name with a virtuous and meritorious meaning is extremely important for Muslim societies. The names are usually Arabic, but they need not be so. The Prophet is reported to have said: 'You will be called by your names and the names of your fathers on the Day of Judgement, so give yourselves good names'

('Ulwān 1981: I, 77). The removal of hair and the sacrifice of an animal are acts associated with the protection of the child from unseen forces. Although it is not a common practice, it is also recommended that the bones of the animal sacrificed should not be broken. A modern commentator has suggested that this practice expresses 'a wish and optimism for the health and strength of the bones of the child, because the sacrifice is a form of expiation for the child' ('Ulwān 1981: I, 98). This statement gives us a sense of the original significance of the sacrifice that restores order and health after the precarious moments of childbirth. On the other hand, the celebration of birth is also an occasion to affirm the social community that the new child is entering, and the sacrifice provides an opportunity to spell out such a unity around a meal.

Wherever possible, two sheep or goats should be sacrificed for a boy and one for a girl. This follows attributed traditions of the Prophet, which apparently contradict the principle in the Qur'ān that chastises men who grieve at the birth of a daughter. There seems to have been a difference of opinion among the jurists on this matter. Most schools follow this discriminatory rule, but the school of Mālik, based on a Prophetic statement and the practice of a prominent companion of the Prophet, 'Abd Allah b. 'Umar, recommends otherwise. For the Mālikī school there should be no distinction between the birth of male and female in the matter of sacrifice ('Ulwān 1981: I, 94–5). This is a small indication that there were many issues, covering both beliefs and rituals, that were open to debate in early Islam. The place of women in Islam will be dealt with more extensively in this study, and it will be opportune to remember then this gender significance in the birth sacrifice.

The next important stage of a person's life takes place at puberty. Physical puberty marks an official entry point from childhood to adult status. In religious terms, all Muslims who have attained puberty are expected to perform their regular daily worship, to fast in the month of Ramadan, to pay the poor-due if they possess the required amount of excess wealth and to undertake the journey to Mecca. There is no official ritual in terms of jurisprudence to designate such an adult status, but graduation from elementary religious schools often marks such a transition. For many children, the complete recitation of the Qur'ān becomes a kind of initiation into adult status. In some African societies, Muslims participate in elaborate traditional initiation ceremonies and adapt them to Islamic demands. In this as in many other situations, the Islamic demands on local cultures are quite flexible. Islamic jurisprudence sets the religious demands, but allows communities to govern how such demands will be accommodated.

An important rite that sometimes takes place at the time of adolescence is circumcision. A *ḥadīth* narrated by Abū Hurayrah, a prominent companion of the Prophet Muhammad, places circumcision in the broader framework of what may be characterized as personal hygiene: 'Five things are part of the natural state of being human: circumcision, shaving the pubes, shaving under the armpits, trimming the moustache, and cutting the nails' (quoted in Sābiq 1980: I, 34). There are basically two positions on circumcision in Islam. Some scholars maintain that circumcision is a Prophetic practice for men, but not necessarily compulsory. This group, moreover, states that circumcision is only recommended as an ennobling practice for women. The particular justification for this position is captured in the statement of one of the protagonists, al-Ḥasan al-Baṣrī: 'Many people became Muslim with the Messenger of God: the black, the white, the Roman, the Persian, and the Ethiopian. And none of them were circumcised' ('Ulwān 1981: I, 103). For this group, it seems that circumcision and its ritual was not a mark of belonging to a community. As a result, the practice was only a recommendation from a legal point of view. This particular Islamic position seems to stand midway between the classical Jewish and Christian positions on the issue. It does not make circumcision a distinctive mark of the covenant like the Jewish tradition, nor does it completely reject it as a religious practice, as does Christianity.

But the Islamic position is not univocal on the issue. A second group, basing their authority more on the literal import of reports from the Prophet and his early Companions, come close to the Jewish position on the question. Scholars in this group insist that circumcision is absolutely essential for males. The *ḥadīth* scholar Aḥmad b. Ḥanbal insisted upon circumcision for women as well. The majority of scholars, past and present, however, do not support this latter view, although it is very common in some Muslim communities like the Sudan and countries in West Africa. In recent times many women, both locally and internationally, have begun to oppose this practice for its inhumanity and mutilation. Unfortunately, it is a practice that continues unabated in some countries, among them some Islamic communities.

Two types of justifications seem to guide those who state that circumcision is absolutely essential in Islam. The jurist Mālik said: 'A person who has not been circumcised may not become a prayer leader, and his testimony is not acceptable' ('Ulwān 1981: I, 103). This particular position seems to employ circumcision as a boundary mechanism between Muslims and others. In support of this approach, a statement attributed to the Prophet is clear and emphatic: 'Throw off the hair of disbelief and circumcise!' (*ibid.*). This remark was directed at someone who had become a Muslim. It is clear that one of the important functions of circumcision is to distinguish belief from disbelief, and one would expect the act itself to become an important ritual to mark that transition. For persons born within the Muslim community, circumcision rites sometimes echo the adolescence rites in African religions. An example of this is in the ceremony that accompanies circumcision in Moroccan society. On the other hand, circumcision also plays an important function for converts, essentially male, entering the Islamic faith. Medical doctors perform the rite in a clinical operation, marking the entry into the new religious community. The question of how women enter the community is not usually the subject of much of this male-dominated discussion.

In recent times, a second justification for circumcision has emerged. Without rejecting the religious justification, contemporary writers focus on the health benefits of circumcision. They argue that circumcision is associated with a reduced chance of urinary infection. To that extent, it is recommended that circumcision should be performed at an early age. Moreover, Islam's less emphatic insistence on circumcision is taken to be one of the secrets of its jurisprudence, in that it reflects the lesser benefits of female circumcision ('Ulwan 1981: I, 107, 109). In general, the argument for circumcision tends to incorporate its assumed physical benefits. This particular approach does not seem to be reflected in the earliest records, but it may be related to the meaning of *fiṭrah* in the *ḥadīth* quoted at the beginning of the discussion: 'Five things are part of the natural state of being human (*fiṭrah*): circumcision, shaving the pubes, shaving under the armpits, trimming the moustache, and cutting the nails.' Each of these actions is closely associated with a discipline in bodily comportment and personal hygiene clearly related to how a believer regarded his relationship with God. Circumcision, which comes at the head of the list, plays an important role in this regard. If the meaning of *fiṭrah* in the statement is concerned with personal body hygiene, then one may include toilet etiquette, using perfume, and other important details in the daily life of Muslims that reinforce the importance of purity in Islam. It is this sense of purity and cleanliness that many contemporary Muslims, particularly those concerned about the reform of Muslim society, regard as the sine qua non of Islam. The justification for circumcision also originates from such quarters.

The next stage in a person's Islamic life is related to marriage, another important institution. Young Muslims are encouraged to marry young or practise abstinence. In one well-known *ḥadīth* the Prophet recommends young people who cannot control their sexual appetite, and who are not in a position to get married, to fast as much as possible. On the other hand, arranged marriages are not encouraged. In all cases, the consent of both men and women is absolutely essential. Even in the context of the absolute separation of the sexes in traditional Islamic societies, prospective marriage couples may get to know each other to a limited extent.

The marriage ceremony itself is a simple affair that usually takes place in a mosque, but could take place elsewhere. The basic requirements are that it should be a public event, and announced to the entire community. The person presiding over the marriage leads the groom and the bride into a marriage contract governed by the requirements of Islamic jurisprudence. A guardian who has obtained the bride's consent usually represents her at the ceremony. Only in rare cases does the woman directly take part in the actual marriage ceremony. The marriage must be accompanied by a gift (*mahr*) to the bride, which can sometimes be an enormous amount of money. The gift, however, is the absolute property of the bride. If the gift is a large sum of money, it may even be deferred to a later date. In this way, the husband may begin their marriage contract with a debt owed to his wife. Marriage is not a sacrament in Islam, and divorce is not an anathema. Of course, this does not mean that divorce is encouraged. A statement of the Prophet describes it as the most hateful of things permitted by God.

The marriage ceremony itself is very simple and short, but it is followed by a grand celebration that differs from culture to culture. In pure Islamic terms, the Prophetic recommendation is to hold a celebration, called the *walīmah*, upon the consummation of the marriage, inviting as many people as possible to celebrate the making of a new family. In traditional Muslim societies the celebration is sometimes distorted when the consummation feast becomes directly dependent on the evidence of the virginity of the bride. The celebration for the new couple is diverted into a conquest over female virginity.

The final rite of passage, the funeral, is also an important event in a Muslim's life. Death is regarded as a sleep: 'How do you deny God and you were dead and he gave you life? Again will he cause you to die and bring you to life again. Then, you shall be brought back to him' (Qur'ān 2:28). Sleep is a metaphor of death, which is thereby made an unthreatening and ordinary event. For each person, moreover, death will take place at an appointed time after he or she has lived a fixed period of time (*ajal*). There is a finality and determinism in death which Muslims accept with quiet dignity. Death is the will of God, whether it takes in a car accident, a hospital or on the battlefield.

The funeral service of a Muslim is informal and simple in the extreme. As soon as a person dies, preparations must begin for burial. Professional undertakers are still rare, and friends and neighbours open their purses and their hearts to assist. According to a well-known *ḥadīth*, attending the funeral of a Muslim is regarded as one of the five obligations that Muslims owe each other: 'Five rights are owed by one Muslim to another: to return his greeting, to visit him when ill, to follow his funeral, to respond to his invitation, and to bless him when he sneezes' ('Ulwān 1981: I, 418). A funeral service forms part of an intricate social web of relationships covering minor and major social obligations. The corpse is given a ritual bath and then placed in a shroud of two pieces of cloth. It is recommended that the corpse be perfumed as well. The recitation of the Qur'ān plays an important part in the bereaved household. Each person visiting the home traditionally recites a portion for the soul of the deceased. A special funeral prayer (*janāzah*) is performed over the deceased, who is then taken to the cemetery. It is recommended that, wherever possible, the bier is carried there. That is why it is not uncommon to witness long processions, sometimes on foot, winding through the streets of a Muslim community. At the cemetery itself, the prepared corpse is placed in the grave with its face turned towards Mecca. No casket is used, but the body is placed in a slight recess in the direction of Mecca. A series of wooden planks are placed over the body before the grave is covered. It is particularly meritorious to be granted the responsibility of placing the corpse in the grave. Usually, close friends or family members do this. A closing supplication usually concludes the funeral rite.

The rites of passage form an important map of transition points in the life of a believer. From birth to death, these rites are sometimes more significant for understanding a culture or religion than the theological and religious teachings expounded by specialists. As ritual acts, they tend to display the values of the religion in a concrete manner. Ritual acts, however, can also be habitual acts that do not contain the changes and tensions in theologies or philosophies propounded by authorities at any given point of time. As much as they can display the values and principles of a culture, they also display the remnants of earlier ideas which are no longer relevant. Thus, for example, the removal of a baby's hair at birth may originally be related to notions of magic and superstition that now affect fewer Muslims than before. The practice is carried out as a recommendation from the Prophet, but its actual significance is buried in history.

THE *NAFS* AND SELF-CONTROL

Reinhart has identified a key ethical concept in Islamic purification rites which merits further discussion. This is the concept of self-mastery that lies at the heart of purification rituals, and also at the centre of Islam's understanding of the human condition. The human self, called the *nafs* in Arabic, has the capacity to turn towards God and purity or to become the 'lowest of the low' (Qur'ān 95:5). Both these capacities have been granted by God: 'By the self and how He has granted it due proportion. He has granted it the capacity to transgress and to be God-conscious' (Qur'ān 91:7–8). Human beings find themselves between these two forces: they can respond to God, and do good, or they can follow their lower capacities, and descend to the deepest levels of immorality.

Iblis, the chief Satan in Islamic belief, desperately tried to subvert the virtuous nature of humanity. He and his minions, collectively called Satans in the Qur'ān, tried desperately to trick humans into forgetting or ignoring their potentially good characteristics, and to lead them to damnation. In the Islamic narrative of the origins of humankind, when the first individual (Adam) was created, God asked angels to bow down to him. Among all those present, only Iblis refused, because he believed that he was better than Adam. God then threw him out of the divine presence where he had attained high rank, but Iblis promised that he would not give up tempting Adam and his progeny: 'Certainly, I will sit in ambush for them on your [God's] path; then come upon them from the front and the back, from the right and the left. And you will not find too many thankful to you' (Qur'ān 7:16–17). The stratagems of Iblis took many forms, and humankind had to be constantly on its guard.

One of the most powerful symbols in this human struggle to gain mastery over the self revolved around the Islamic understanding of the world. The planet on which humans live is called the *al-arḍ* (the earth), but this refers to its physical features. Human habitation, culture and civilization transform the physical properties of the world as animate and inanimate location. Now, the earth becomes a human habitat of meaning and significance. In the Qur'ān, the earth (*al-arḍ*) can be distinguished from life on earth (*al-ḥayāt al-dunyā*). The former refers to the plants, trees, animals, water and its many other resources, while *al-ḥayāt al-dunyā* refers to the human interaction with it. This latter is a powerful symbol, which literally means the 'immediate life'. Often referred to by its adjective as *dunyā*, the concept conjures a multitude of meanings in the Islamic conception of human life on earth. Usually negative, *al-dunyā* stands in contrast to *al-ākhirah*, short for *al-ḥayah al-ākhirah*, which means 'the other life' or 'deferred life'. *Al-dunyā* and *al-ākhirah* are binary opposites in Islam, corresponding to the pairs of right and left; good and evil; immediate and deferred; saved and damned. In terms of the concept of self-mastery, the *dunyā* represents the value which is close at hand, and which seems convenient and tempting. It is, however, the deferred and the controlled sentiment that must be sought by human beings. They cannot, and should not, be tempted by the immediate gains and gratification of the *dunyā*, but must develop the patience to strive for the greater reward which is deferred in the *ākhirah*.

Sometimes this approach to the world has very easily lent itself to extreme denial and asceticism. Many of the early mystics in Islam interpreted the world as a prison, a place from which one must escape. For them, the Qur'ānic rejection of the *dunyā* was a call to asceticism and self-denial. Thus, sometimes in their reflections, which continue to influence Muslim attitudes today, this world (*al-dunyā*) took on extremely negative connotations. Some examples will clarify their approach:

> He is a wise man who regards this world as nothing, and so regarding it, seeks the other world, instead of setting at naught the other world and seeking this. Whoso knows God regards Him as a friend and whoso knows this world regards Him as an enemy.
>
> (Ḥasan al-Baṣrī (d. 728); quoted in Smith 1950: 8)

> Avoid covetousness by preferring contentment: make sure of the sweetness of asceticism by cutting short hope; destroy motives to desire by despairing altogether of the creatures; secure peace of mind by trust in God; extinguish the fires of desire by the coldness of despair; close the road to pride by the knowledge of assured faith; seek peace of body by

> finding rest for the heart; secure peace of mind through ceasing to contend and abandoning the search for one's own good.
>
> (Abū 'Abdallah Abū Bakr 'Āṣim al-Anṭākī (d. 835); quoted in Smith 1950: 12–13)

One should therefore guard against the world as *dunyā*, the sum total of immediate gratification. According to Andrae, for the early Sufis, 'the world is thus a concept which, is, in the final analysis, religiously determined. What the world is, its value or worthlessness, is determined solely in terms of our relationship with God' (Andrae 1987: 69). In this regard, the body as the locus of material gratification was part of the world (*dunyā*). As a locus for desire and material gratification, the body became the pivotal concept of the *dunyā*. It was regarded as a product of this world, and worthy of rejection. Only the spirit, the true nature of the self, had the potential to produce human salvation.

It should be noted that we are here talking about *dunyā* and not the earth as nature and creation of God. When it comes to the latter, the Sufis extended the Qur'ānic symphony of the signs of nature in their poetry and prose. Again, Andrae cites the lyrical songs of Dhū 'l-Nūn (d. *c.* 859):

> O God, whenever I listen to the voices of the animals, to the wind in the tree and the song of the birds; whenever I enjoy the coolness of shade, listen to the howling storm and raging thunder, in all this I find a testimony to Thy goodness.
>
> (Andrae 1987: 69)

The believer had to balance between the world defined by its conceptual construction, always potentially ensnaring, and the sign of God, which was liberating. From one angle, the world was a sign of God taking the mystic to his beloved. From another perspective, involvement in the world distracted him or her from the real goal. For a proper evaluation of the Islamic conception of the world, we must take into consideration this perspectival shift between the physical world and its human appropriation. The world, as reality and nature, was part of the wonderful creation of God and suggested signs and moments for the true reflection of God. The world, as the product of human relation apart from God, was potentially dangerous.

Against these early Sufis, however, it should be noted that other scholars argued for a more moderate position towards the *dunyā*.

Extreme asceticism was regarded as a misunderstanding of the true meaning of Islam's attitude to the world and the human body. Islam was a world-affirming religion, and regulated the relations of human beings therein. In fact, the very use of *dunyā* and *ākhirah* in the Qur'ān is interestingly subtle in its reference to the play between 'now' and 'immediate' on the one hand, and 'later' and 'deferred' on the other. In an early chapter of the Qur'ān, the Prophet Muhammad is consoled for the persecution he suffered at the hands of his Meccan opponents. In this context, he is told to be patient since 'the deferred (*ākhirah*) will be better than the earlier (*al-ūlā*)' (Qur'ān 93:4). In this verse, the word *al-ākhirah* meant both the end of time with God, and a later time within history. Situated within the context of Prophetic history, the chapter in the Qur'ān promised that the believers would eventually overcome their opponents, as did happen with the conquest of Mecca and the establishment of Islam as a political and economic power in Arabia. Another world-affirming verse in the Qur'ān reminds humans 'not to forget their share of the *dunyā*' (Qur'ān 28: 77). Thus, as a religion on which polities and empires were built, Islam does not believe that all Islamic virtue is to be postponed for the hereafter. In general, the self-mastery of human beings over the *dunyā* was not so much a complete denial as the 'control' to which Reinhart referred. Wealth, marriage, children and other pleasures in the *dunyā* could well become a distraction, but the trick was to exercise restraint and control. A well-known maxim said that faith should be in your heart and the world in your pocket: you should keep faith, but be prepared to do without the world. The inverse was dangerous as far as ultimate salvation was concerned, and short-sighted as far as ethics was concerned. Thus the two views may be placed on a continuum reaching from a distinction between world and earth to that between world/earth and the hereafter. The former, generally represented by the mystics, revealed a constant struggle to see the truth being unveiled; the latter regarded the goal as an ethical quest to establish priorities.

FASTING

It may be appropriate to conclude this chapter with a brief discussion of fasting in Islam as this takes asceticism and self-control to its logical conclusion. Fasting takes place during the month of Ramadan, the ninth month in the lunar calendar. Since the lunar calendar is slightly shorter than the solar calendar, the month of fasting moves through the seasons. The end of the Ramadan is concluded with a special festival, the 'Īd al-Fiṭr, the festival of fast-breaking. Fasting in Ramadan is considered to be one of the fundamental pillars of Islam. It is a systematic denial of food, drink and sexual relations from before daybreak until sunset. During this time, all adult Muslims who are not ill, menstruating, travelling, or otherwise incapacitated must impose these restrictions upon themselves. In many Muslim communities young children also join in and abstain as much as they can.

The practice of fasting is a temporary reversal of the regular order of everyday life. The human relationship with food, in this case a powerful symbol of the world and its evanescence, is brought into sharp relief in this month. The denial during fasting is not total, but it is a sufficiently disorienting experience, which Muslims are urged to take advantage of to attain *taqwā* (God-consciousness). The following verse in the Qur'ān establishes the reason for fasting: 'O you who believe, fasting has been prescribed for you as it was prescribed to those before so that you may attain *taqwā*' (Qur'ān 2:183). The ritual of fasting is thus not unique to Muslims. It is a universal practice, involving learning control and self-restraint. In Islamic terms, the most profound goal of self-restraint is *taqwā*. This concept connotes a sense of fear, awe and reverence in the presence of God. When the second caliph 'Umar asked Ubayy b. Ka'b the meaning of the term, the latter presented to him a vivid image of the concept: '"Have you ever walked through a field of thorn bushes?" Umar replied, "Yes." Ka'b asked: "What did you do?" "I lifted my clothes and was careful." And he said: "That is *taqwā*."' (Qutb 1980: I, 39). Fasting is an ideal opportunity for attaining this state of heightened awareness, as one foregoes the normal routine of life and temporarily suspends one's natural bodily urges. In this case, one becomes highly conscious of good and evil as one charts a path through life. Furthermore, the practice of fasting is especially meritorious because the act is not normally evident to the observer, thus reducing the possibility of pious show. Thus, recognizing the selfless nature of fasting, the Prophet is reported to have said: 'God said, Fasting is for me, and I will personally grant reward for it' (Sābiq 1980: I, 400). Distinct from other form of worship, fasting need not be performed in public; it is a state of being known only to God and the fasting person.

In Ramadan, moreover, the process of introspection is carried further during the nights. Of course, in many instances, abstinence is followed by extreme consumption and sometimes revelry. Twentieth-century Cairo has been described as a carnival during the nights of Ramadan. In religious terms, however, the nights of Ramadan are no less auspicious. They are filled with additional prayer and recitation of the Qur'ān. The latter becomes particularly significant, as Muslims believe that the Qur'ān was brought down during this month from the seventh heaven on to the first heaven. The seventh heaven symbolizes the divine realm, while the first heaven symbolizes the human realm. The Qur'ān celebrates this event as the Night of Power.

> We have brought it down on the Night of Power.
> And what will explain to you what is the Night of Power?
> The Night of Power is greater than a thousand months
> In it, the angels and the Spirit descend with the permission
> of their Lord on every affair
> Peace it is until the break of dawn.
>
> (Qur'ān 97:1–5)

In commemoration of this event, the Qur'ān is recited continuously. Additional cycles of worship after the regular night prayer, called *tarāwīḥ*, provide an opportunity for reciting the entire Qur'ān in congregation.

And then, towards the end of the month, many Muslims seek the miracle of another auspicious night in the Islamic calendar. In conformity with the Prophet's statement that anybody may be able to experience the Night of Power, Muslims spend many nights of vigil in devotion, recitation of the Qur'ān and general contemplation. Numerous Prophetic reports suggest that the auspicious night is likely to fall within the last ten days of Ramadan, on an odd night most probably, or, for those who only have one night to spare, the twenty-seventh night. Muslims engage in prayer and devotion in order to experience the power of God, or at least to catch a glimpse of the power of temporary seclusion. The Night of Power, the night on which the Qur'ān was revealed, is regarded as a gift given to Muslims in order that they may be able to gain some notion of how the two worlds of earth and heaven touch. Since the Qur'ān is in some way a symbol of that meeting, the Night of Power makes that possible for those chosen few who are prepared to seek it. And it is quite fitting that it should fall in Ramadan, a month when the highest degree of control and vigilance has been created. Rūmī regarded the Night of Power as the pre-eminent symbol of being in the presence of God, an experience that we yearn for from our usual solitary and empty lives:

> Union with Him is the Night of Power, separation from
> Him the night of the grave
> The night of the grave sees miraculous generosity and
> replenishment from the Night of Power.
>
> (Quoted in Chittick 1983: 233)

Walking into the mosque's ablution facility provided us with an opportunity to consider the place and meaning of purification in Islam. We began first with purification of the body and moved on to its implication for conceptual purity. The two, we found, were inextricably linked. The comparative approach to the study of religion allowed us to pursue the cosmological significance of the self and the world, while Islamic jurisprudence placed purification within the context of a systematic theory of human acts. The latter became a convenient occasion to explore the early development of jurisprudence, and its relation with political power. The chapter concluded with fasting in Islam, which is fittingly connected with the purification of the self. Within that experience, the Night of Power moves to the climax of experiencing the meeting of heaven and earth. The Night of Power represents that pinnacle of religious experience for which symbols, values and images yearn.

3 THE INTERIOR OF THE MOSQUE
Space, gender dynamics and aesthetics

One step further into the mosque, and we come into the central space for prayer and meditation. Following our discussion on the associated metaphors of the minaret and the ablution blocks in the last two chapters, the interior space of the mosque helps us to explore further dimensions of Islam. As in all religions, the notion of space in Islam plays an important role in the life of Muslims. One speaks with difficulty about sacred space, in the sense of the sacred or the divine descending and occupying a place on earth. Such a notion would go against the Islamic theological doctrine which insists on the utter otherness of God. As the Qur'ānic verse emphasizes: 'There is nothing like unto him' (Qur'ān 42:11). However, if religious space is regarded more loosely as the product of rituals and narratives, and less as the presence or absence of beings, then Islamic space becomes more meaningful and amenable to analysis and appreciation. In this sense, space is constantly being created and shaped through acts: some spaces are accorded more importance than others, and some regarded as being in closer proximity to important events. In this chapter, the inner space of the mosque will be used to explore this latter notion of space in Islam. This will be followed with some discussion of the gender dynamics of space in Islam, and by extension, in society. The chapter will take advantage of being inside the mosque to explore the meaning of art in Islam.

THE WORLD IS A MOSQUE

It is reported that the Prophet Muhammad said that the 'earth was made pure and a place of prostration for me; wherever a person finds himself at the time of prayer, let him pray' (Ibn Ḥajar n.d.). The Prophet mentioned this in the context of a distinguishing feature of his prophecy, and thus a distinguishing feature of the religion of Islam. From an Islamic point of view, the earth is considered pure, a creation of God, and thus worthy of prayer and prostration to its creator. Of course, this has not prevented Muslims from producing and building great monuments in mosque architecture. However, the fundamental principle within Islam lay in the adoption of the earth as a place of prostration. The renowned scholar of Islamic mysticism, Seyyed Hossein Nasr, regards the earth and nature as the 'primordial mosque' emulated by mosques in Islamic cities and towns (Nasr 1990: 10).

This conviction that the earth is a mosque may be seen in many Muslim contexts. In conformity with the statement of the Prophet Muhammad, it is not unusual to see Muslims simply rolling out a carpet anywhere they find themselves and proceeding to fulfil their obligation to God at the appointed time of the day or night. The image of a lonely worshipper in a vast empty desert has been exploited by many a film-maker. More recently, this observance of the earth as a mosque can be seen on the part of modern travellers in some of the world's busiest airports. Often these images pay little attention to the actual movements involved in prayer, but they do succeed in illustrating that Muslims do not require a formal place of worship in order to fulfil their commitment to God. In jurisprudence, the same belief about the mosque may be appreciated in scholars' insistence that buildings set aside for prayer should have no strings attached. Such a structure is only considered a mosque if the builder or the donor relinquishes ownership. The Qur'ānic verse 'And to God belong the mosques' (72:18) became the cornerstone for ensuring that mosque endowments were completely unencumbered. This was a juridical and legal way in which to preserve, or perhaps restore, the natural state of the mosque. In this pure, non-owned status, the mosque could only belong to God in a way that everything else on earth does and should do.

In early Islamic jurisprudence, the Imāmī Shi'ites exemplified the same principle in a slightly different, but equally emphatic manner. These jurists insisted that at least the prostration should be performed on a piece of pure earth in conformity with the practice of the Prophet. In fact, they argued that this was also the preferred practice among some of the early Sunni jurists (al-Ḥilli n. d.: I, 91). As Imāmī Shi'ite jurisprudence expanded, scholars elaborated on whether one might prostrate on the products of the earth as well. Generally, it was concluded that the earth, and anything that grew on it, was acceptable, but that it was not permissible to pray on food, clothing or minerals. As is clear, jurisprudence developed its own logic on the basis of formal precedent, and the practice of using a piece of stone or ground for prostration may have became somewhat obscured. At the very least, it has become a ritual emblem marking off Shi'ism from Sunnism. Some Sunnis even privately suspect that Shi'ites worship the ground of Karbala in Iraq, where the grandson of the Prophet fell, and which is preferred in popular Shi'ite practice. However, a study of the earliest sources reveals that the use of the piece of ground is closely related to the principle that the earth itself was the original mosque. The fundamental principle emphasized that the earth as a place of prostration was a special gift bestowed by God on the Prophet Muhammad and his followers. We saw in the first chapter how the loudspeaker became an expanded symbol in modern Islam: this also happened with the stone used for prostration in Shi'ism.

Whilst the earth everywhere was a mosque, this did not mean the complete elimination of special and distinguished places in Islam. As in other religions, certain places on the earth were accorded greater status. Their historical and ritual importance within Islam gave them a degree of eminence. This tension between the special and the general is captured eloquently in the following statement of al-Jazā'irī in his compendium of comparative Sunni jurisprudence:

> Islamic *Sharī'ah* does not give greater eminence to one place over another. The relative merit of places is like the relative merit among people in reference to a non-material distinction. Thus, the merit of one mosque over another is in reference to religious and literary events that took place in one, and not the other. Thus, the Sacred Mosque in Mecca is the centre of the Ka'bah towards which God has ordered Muslims to worship in a special way. Likewise, the Prophetic Mosque in Medina has special merit for the events which took place therein, such as the descent of revelation and for its central role in which the leaders of Islam learnt the principle of Islam on the authority of the Prophet.
>
> (al-Jazā'irī n. d.: I, 291)

Thus, while sacrality that is inherent in a place poses a continuing problem, three places in Islam stand out for special consideration in terms of their historical and ritual eminence. The highest prestige in the Islamic spatial framework is accorded to the Sacred Mosque in Mecca, to which all Muslims turn in worship. By turning to Mecca in prayer, Muslims the world over conferred upon it a 'sacred' character. Similarly, the eminence of Medina follows Mecca because the Prophet Muhammad established his community there, and because it became the centre of religious devotion and study. The Farthest Mosque in Jerusalem is special because it was the home of previous prophets, as well as being the first direction for worship for the early Muslim community. Notwithstanding the disclaimer in al-Jazā'irī's statement, therefore, these places have also been accorded esteemed, almost sacred, characteristics in Islamic discourse. In other narratives of Islam, the Meccan sanctuary is regarded as the first place of worship, established by Adam and then again by Abraham. In cosmological terms, it stands directly under the throne of God. Just as angels circumambulate the latter, human beings perform similar rituals on the earth. Stories and narratives in other Muslim contexts have recreated the importance of these places, investing sacral connections in them and inspiring numerous travels and pilgrimages.

Apart from these eminent mosques, Islamic jurisprudence has also defined religious space in towns, villages and cities. In jurisprudence, the subject of the mosque is part of the subject of prayer. At a basic level, jurists simply required that the place where the prayer is performed should be free of defiling substances like urine and faeces. The issue becomes more complicated, and simultaneously more illuminating, when the subject of the Friday prayer comes up. It is here that Islamic jurisprudence defined the Friday mosque as an expression of a community. While ordinary congregational worship may be valid if performed by two individuals, Friday worship could only take place with the support of all the people in a wider locality. The central mosque, located often in the capital city or in the most important cities in a country, was called the *jāmi'* and was distinct from the *masjid*. The latter was any place where regular congregational prayers were performed, while the former became the important symbol of Muslims in a country or region. Early Islamic thinking thus insisted that people living in small villages had to join the cities. They also suggested, and sometimes insisted, that all people in one city ought to pray together in one place; that there ought to be at least forty worshippers present; and that the Friday prayer could not be performed in the open. The stipulations have often been made more complex as law ramified into many areas.

From the perspective of how space is defined, these rules show the interrelationship between space and a community. What emerges from these stipulations is the creation of a Friday congregational space wherein the community came together. The group, the city, and unity among Muslims seem of paramount importance. Among the earlier schools, and certainly in the Shi'ite tradition, the Friday congregation could not even go ahead without the permission of the ruler. Friday congregational worship was thus also the expression of a political community, and not simply a religious community occupying a particular piece of ground.

With the spread of Islam, the emergence of very large cities, and political problems within the Islamic polity, the definition of Friday congregational worship, and by implication its space, underwent a transformation. Thus, the requirement for permission from the ruler, among Sunni schools at least, was dropped. As time progressed, and as rulers seemed less and less to reflect righteous conduct, their permission became a shallow formality as far as the practice of the religion was concerned. Some schools even ceased to require it altogether. Jurisprudence seemed to be keeping up with the increasingly diversified nature of the Muslim community, the *ummah*. This does not mean that the central mosque in the capital, or in the palace, lost all importance. As a mouthpiece of the reigning political ruler, such a mosque continued to espouse the sometimes tenuous legitimacy of the ruler. The Friday sermon was obliged to acknowledge the reigning caliph, and sometimes became a signal during periods of political instability. When a preacher stopped mentioning the name of a prevailing ruler or substituted it with another, it was an indication that the palace inhabitants had changed. Clearly, the mosque now became simply the site from which the political fortunes of the elite were announced. In general though, we may still speak of a mosque as a religious site which expressed, through ritual and rules, the aspirations and desires of a community.

In modern times, the requirement for one single Friday service in a city has also been dropped. This trend has accelerated as cities have grown through urbanization and new migrations. Thus, until 1970, the city of Kano in Nigeria had only one Friday mosque, and it took some time to convince the scholars to agree to another. When they eventually did, their agreement led to a series of mosques being built in the increasingly burgeoning city. Mosques in contemporary Islamic cities usually serve the interests of ruling political regimes, and their leaders are carefully chosen for the purpose. In countries where the political stakes of the Friday congregational service are not as high, however, the *jāmi'* may also play a key role in the symbolization of Islamic presence. For example, the Regent's Park Mosque in London, situated in the heart of the city, aspires to duplicate the symbolic role of the Friday congregational mosque. In other towns and cities where no political or religious authority lays claims to a mosque, an unspoken eminence is granted to the earliest, the biggest or the most influential mosque as the *jāmiʿ*.

Sometimes, Friday worship defines the power map of an Islamic community in terms of space. An example of this is found in nineteenth-century Cape Town, where Muslims had established numerous mosques, often in competition with each other. At the end of the century, they began to explore ways of selecting one mosque as the Friday mosque for the entire community. This particular requirement to have one Friday mosque is especially emphatic in the Shāfiʿī school of law, which most Muslims in Cape Town followed. In terms of Shāfiʿī law, a single *jumuʿah* (Friday congregational service) should be performed for all the inhabitants of an urban area. If multiple services were carried out only the earliest one was really valid. The rest were obliged to perform the usual midday prayer (*ẓuhr*) in addition to the Friday prayer. As far as the Cape Town mosques were concerned, the candidates included the Awwal Mosque, founded at the end of the previous century, a *jāmiʿ* founded in the middle of the nineteenth century, and numerous other mosques, all claiming to hold the people in the city together. In the midst of such competing claims, the problem could not be resolved, even after a delegation from Zanzibar tried to find a solution in a roster in which *imāms* from different mosques would take turns to lead the prayers at the Awwal Mosque. The problem was not finding a suitable venue: the search for a single *jumuʿah* exposed the challenge of defining Islamic leadership in the absence of an Islamic state authority. The *jumuʿah* issue was a proxy battle for leadership. In the twentieth century, this same issue of *jumuʿah* and *ẓuhr* also arose in Uganda, Malawi and Madagascar, each time without an amicable solution being found. In each case, the issue of a Friday mosque arose in the context of leadership contested around the nature of a Friday place of worship. This raises many other issues, but for the purpose of our discussion it is sufficient to note that the political and social definition of a religious community was intermeshed with the definition of a mosque, the quintessential symbol of such a community.

It would, however, be a mistake to assume that political and social battles exhaust the nature of a mosque and its space. It is not surprising to find that Islamic jurists, in particular, also defined the mosque space in terms of other rituals, by what one may or may not do inside it. In this way, a different understanding of a mosque emerges. Thus, reflecting the primitive natural mosques of early times, one was not allowed to spit in a forward direction. If you really had to, then the side was better for such a purpose. Sleeping, passing through, raising one's voice, buying and selling, and even decoration of the mosque walls, were frowned upon. The latter is significant, in that mosques are often associated with exquisitely beautiful calligraphy and arabesque decoration, yet, there is some agreement among jurists that this is better left out (al-Jazā'irī n. d.: I, 288). The general principle guiding these regulations, including the absence of decorations, is an attempt to create a space for unhindered devotion. Not even the name of God on a mosque wall should come between the worshipper and his or her concentration upon God. This absolute devotional aspect of the mosque is a means by which space is set aside. Assigning rules of behaviour, then, was a means by which the mosque became a religious space, a space set apart from other spaces. It is the closest that one gets to the notion of a sacred space in Islam. While observers have been correct to repeat the fact that the distinction between sacred and profane in the form of attendant divine beings was not amenable to investigation in Islam, they have often overlooked the creative means by which certain spaces are constructed as accentuated regions and places for devotion. Rules and regulations create this distinctive space, and this kind of space is certainly present in Islam, unlike the valueless world of physics defined by co-ordinates on a Cartesian plane.

This brings us to the actual worship or prayer in Islam that takes place inside the mosque. Muslims believe that regular worship (*ṣalāh*) is a gift for making contact with God. Unlike other forms of religious obligation mentioned in the Qur'ān, *ṣalāh* was presented to the Prophet Muhammad in a special night journey and ascension. Some time during the initial period of his prophetic life in Mecca, the angel Gabriel approached him as he lay in the Meccan sacred sanctuary, and nudged him awake. He then led the Prophet outside where a wonderful winged steed called Burāq was waiting to take him on a journey. Together, they travelled to Jerusalem, where Muhammad led a congregation of prophets in worship, after which he and Gabriel ascended towards the heavens. They crossed seven heavens until they reached the furthest tree, beyond which even Gabriel could not go. Muhammad then crossed the threshold by himself into the divine presence where, as the Qur'ān says, 'his sight did not swerve nor exceed' (Qur'ān 53: 17). On his departure, God granted the Prophet the gift of *ṣalāh*, which had to be performed fifty times a day. Fortunately, on his descent he met Moses, who persuaded Muhammad to return to God and ask for a reduction of the onerous religious obligation. After many such trips, Muhammad eventually returned to earth with five compulsory prayers. And so it has come to pass that Muslims worship five times a day. For many, this seems a great burden, but in Muslim self-understanding it was a gift lightened through the intervention of Moses.

Notwithstanding the charming conclusion, the narrative clearly establishes *ṣalāh* as originating in the spiritual experience of Muhammad. *Ṣalāh* may justifiably be regarded as the supreme form of devotion and obedience to God. While many a *ṣalāh* does not come close to this ideal, the definition of a mosque as a place of prostration tries to create a spatial and temporal context in which such an ideal may be sought and realized. The actual performance of the *ṣalāh* facilitates this achievement in two dimensions. In the first instance, the five *ṣalāh* are performed at appointed times of the day, after which they are also named: *fajr* or *subḥ* before sunrise; *ẓuhr* soon after noon; *'aṣr* in the late afternoon; *maghrib* at sunset; and *'īshā'* when it is completely dark. On Fridays, the *jumu'ah*, literally 'gathering', replaces the *ẓuhr*. Special forms of *ṣalāh* are performed for petitioning God for rain; on the occasion of solar and lunar eclipses; for personal requests and devotion; and during the two festivals (*'īd*s) and Ramadan. *Ṣalāh* thus punctuates the temporal dimension of a person's existence. There is never an occasion when one is far from thinking about one's next encounter with God. From this perspective, the ascension of the Prophet is not a distant miraculous event; it is an opportunity that comes more frequently than humankind cares to consider.

The second dimension concerns the movements and recitations that constitute the *ṣalāh*. The *ṣalāh* consists of a fixed number of cycles (*raka'āt*), each consisting of six movements: standing with arms folded, bowing at the waist, standing, prostrating and sitting, followed by another prostration. The first standing position is usually the longest, during which various sections from the Qur'ān are recited. The prostration, however, is regarded as the pivotal posture of the *ṣalāh*, when one is closest to God, expressing utter selflessness, devotion and obedience. Thus the bodily movements of the *ṣalāh* provide an opportunity for an individual orientation of devotion and rest in God. Just as the rules of jurisprudence create community and society, *ṣalāh* movements create individual space through bodily gestures. They generate humility and self-awareness of one's own finitude in the presence of God. Time and space are both brought into reverence towards a higher order.

A famous Islamic mystic, known as Abū Yazīd al-Bistāmī (d. 874), is known to have translated the account of the heavenly journey of the Prophet into a metaphorical narrative of his spiritual journey. His real name was Ṭayfūr b. 'Īsā b. Surāshān and his teacher was simply known as Abū 'Alī al-Sindhī. The relationship between al-Bistāmī and al-Sindhī was peculiar: apparently the pupil taught the teacher the reading of the Qur'ān in exchange for the inner secrets of the heart. It is such details that suggest that the mystical doctrines within Islam may owe their origin to Indian influences (al-Sindhī is a noun of place referring to Sind, one of the regions of present-day Pakistan). Abū Yazīd did not write anything, but some 500 of his utterances and statements were handed to Junayd, a great saint from Baghdad. These express Abū Yazīd's deep sense of humility and an extreme form of self-negation: he is reported to have said that a person should reject his self like a 'snake sheds a skin'. Abū Yazīd became notorious among theologians for declaring that the divine resided within himself. He is reported to have uttered statements like 'Glory be to me' for the mystical union he experienced with God. The purpose of raising his name in this context, however, relates to his particular appropriation of the Prophetic night journey. He saw the value of the journey as a model of the spiritual quest. The following passage from one of his visions suggests a mystical interpretation and emulation of the Prophet's own journey:

> While I was asleep, it seemed to me that I ascended to the heavens in quest of God, seeking union with God most glorious, so that I might abide with Him for ever, and I was tested by a trial. God displayed before me gifts of all kinds and offered me dominion over the whole heaven, and yet I turned aside my eyes from this, because I knew that He was testing me thereby, and I turned not towards it, out of reverence for the holiness of my Lord and I said in regard to it all: 'O my Beloved, my desire is other than that which is offered to me.' Then I ascended to the second heaven and saw winged angels, who fly a hundred thousand times each day to the earth, to look upon the saints of God, and their faces shone like the sun. I travelled on and when I had reached the Seventh Heaven, one called unto

> me: 'O Abū Yazīd, stop, stop, for you have reached your goal', but I paid no heed to his words and I pursued my quest.
>
> (Quoted in Smith 1950: 27–8)

The mosque in Islam, then, takes on a number of characteristics as Muslims appropriate it for worship and collective organization. In the first instance, I explored the mosque as a primordial, natural space created and designated by God as an unfettered location for worship and devotion. But the mosque is also the product of collective organization, and takes shape around the different ways in which Muslims organize the human settlements of villages, cities and modern metropolises. Most importantly, the specific form of Islamic worship opens the mosque as a site offering paths to God.

CELEBRATING AND COMMEMORATING

Apart from the prescribed ritual obligations, the mosque is also used to commemorate and celebrate occasions and events in the Islamic calendar. It is not only a place for intense devotion and concentration. As a major assembly forum, it is the site where a number of the annual gatherings take place. Thus, the birthday of the Prophet (Mīlād al-Nabī) is usually celebrated on the twelfth of Rabīʿ al-Awwal, the third month of the Islamic calendar. This is an occasion of great joy, when poetry in honour of the Prophet is recited and wonderful stories of his birth are told. Whilst mystics explore the depths of the ascension of the Prophet, the mosques usually observe it on the twenty-seventh eve of Rajab, the seventh month of the Islamic year. As in the celebration of the birthday of the Prophet, the evening is used as an occasion to remember and recall his great spiritual depth. Moreover, the event emphasizes the crucial role of daily worship in Islam. Another important annual event takes place in Shaʿbān, the eighth month of the Islamic calendar. Some call it *barā'ah* (absolution) because it is said to mark the time when the annual records of the good and bad deeds of every person on earth are sent to God. Since the particular event takes place in the middle of Shaʿbān, on the fifteenth of the month, it is also called *niṣf Shaʿbān* (mid-Shaʿbān). The event provides an opportunity for Muslims to begin again with a clean record. In particular, they may ask each other for forgiveness for both intentional and unintentional transgressions that may have occurred between them. Finally, the other significant event in the calendar, the Night of Power

(Laylat al-Qadr), is observed on the twenty-seventh night of Ramadan, the climax of devotion during the month of fasting.

Every community differs in its observation of these events. In Indian communities men usually attend the mosque for the night worship, which is usually followed by a special *khatam*, a ritual during which a few copies of the Qur'ān, each divided into thirty parts, are distributed for recitation. This is followed by a special sermon for the occasion. The event concludes with sweets, fruits and rose scented milk or water distributed by a wealthy patron, often in fulfilment of a vow. These special nights in the town are known as 'big' nights and they attract huge audiences, often larger than the Friday gathering. They are an important means by which ordinary Muslims are introduced to the fundamental pillars of their religion. Two of them, the birthday celebration of the Prophet and his nocturnal journey, emphasize the importance of the Prophet and the religious community, the *ummah*. Likewise, the *barā'ah* night is a tangible occasion for cementing the bonds of commitment in the community, and the special Night of Power in Ramadan at least reminds believers of the deep spiritual potential that exists in each man and woman.

These are the celebrations and commemorations that span across the cultural and geographical boundaries of Muslim communities. However, many mosques also host local events that express the character and idiosyncrasies of their unique histories. If the mosque was founded by a great Sufi figure, it will also host annual celebrations recalling some its founding moments. The Mouridiyyah mosque of Touba in Senegal is the location for an annual gathering that marks the return from exile of Ahmad Bamba (d. 1927). Bamba founded a Sufi order that eschewed *jihād* (struggle) in its military form, but was still suspected by the French of harbouring hostile intentions. His repeated exile only confirmed his religious eminence for the Senegalese, thousands of whom still celebrate his piety and courage. Thus the mosque and its celebrations signify the community at different levels. The worship and devotion relate Muslims to God; the general celebrations reinforce the order's link with global *ummah*; and the local events concretize its specific place in a regional network.

It must be mentioned here that throughout Islamic history reformist scholars have raised their critical voices against some or all of the celebrations in the mosques. Sometimes they have been critical of the manner in which the events were celebrated, as well as of the inversion of priorities. The particular charge levelled against the celebrations was that they were innovations (*bid'ah*) which were not expressly sanctioned by the Qur'ān or the Prophet. The criticism against innovation is based on the following *hadīth* in which the Prophet is reported to have said: 'He who innovates something in this matter of ours that is not of it will have it rejected' (An-Nawawi 1976: 40). In conformity with such statements, the Qur'ān and Prophetic practice are used as criteria by which popular practices are critiqued and evaluated. Such acts are charged with *bid'ah*, a particularly negative term in Islamic parlance. Since the beginning of Islamic history, the term has been a powerful mechanism by which religious scholars have controlled the practice of religious duties. While creeds and dogmatic formulae have tried to keep beliefs in check, the charge of *bid'ah* relates to practices and rituals. From the eighteenth century, the modern world has witnessed an increase in the number of ritual practices deemed to be *bid'ah*. One of them, the celebration of the birthday of the Prophet, will be the subject of a brief discussion in the light of this.

In spite of the clarity of the ban on innovation, the issue has not been entirely without a fair share of disputation. Some of the early caliphs had introduced a number of changes which seem to contradict the ban on innovations in their entirety. Consequently, there are two positions in Islam on the question of innovations. One completely rejects all forms of innovation, while the second makes a distinction between good and bad innovations. The first is probably best represented by the Damascene scholar Aḥmad b. Taymiyyah (d. 1328), who rejected the scholastic arguments of the theological schools as innovations. Ibn Taymiyyah has a number of contemporary supporters who reject in principle any local customs and traditions observed by Muslims as religious duties or practices. Thus, in our example, the celebration of the birthday of the Prophet (Mīlād al-Nabī) is rejected on such grounds.

In contrast with Ibn Taymiyyah, 'Abd al-Raḥmān al-Suyūṭī (d. 1505) represents a different position on the matter. He made a distinction between types of innovations and justified the celebration of the birthday of the Prophet on the basis of analogy (*qiyās*). Al-Suyūṭī argued that the Prophet fasted on Monday and specifically mentioned that he did so because it was the day on which he was born. On the basis of analogy, the performance of meritorious and devotional acts on the occasion of the Prophet's birthday was also justified (Kaptein 1993: 59). Of course, the practice of celebrating the birthday of the Prophet may have historically emerged for a different purpose. It is clear from the study of

Kaptein, at least, that it was invented by the Shi'ite Fatimid state to bolster its legitimacy with its Sunni populace. For al-Suyūṭī, the first introduction of the practice was not as important as the general principle that some innovations, like the Mīlād, were good and should be distinguished from bad innovations.

The general question for Muslims revolves around the important question of new and changing forms of religious practices. The rejectionists, like Ibn Taymiyyah, wish to keep the practice of Islam on the straight and narrow, which some observers regard as evidence of the tenacity of Islam to resist change and adaptation to local cultures and modernity. It is clear from this brief discussion, however, that a different position within Islam is equally well grounded. This promotes adaptation and is open to the addition of practices without them replacing the fundamental pillars of Islam. The example of the birthday of the Prophet clearly illustrates this flexibility.

Graham sees this tension within Islam as regards ritual change and modification as a mechanism of critical reflection. Islamic ritual, he argues, carried the seed of its own reform (Graham 1983: 63–4). According to Graham, those who rejected innovations ensured the continuity of Islamic practice over the centuries. Extending this line of thought, the history of Islam in a particular culture may be seen as a progressive rejection of local cultures. Thus Fisher argues that the history of Islam in West Africa may be charted along a trajectory that begins with the court and ends with reform. When Islam first entered West African kingdoms, it was represented by healers and advisors in the African court. At this stage, those who became Muslims were not expected to change or modify local practices. However, by the eighteenth century the reform phase had set in, in which local practices were eliminated and Islamic practice purified. While this is the general pattern of Islamic development in the region over five centuries, it must be remembered that this is not necessarily a one-way process. Fisher is careful to point this out (Fisher 1973: 31). When we take into consideration the religious debates and resources of this question, we must recognize who supported adaptation and ensured the relevance of Islam to local cultures and sentiments. Innovation is the mechanism by which a geography- and culture-transcending religion entered into conversation with local practices. The conversation was bound to produce some disputation, and the conclusion was not prefigured in an essentialist position within Islam.

GENDERED SPACE: FROM MOSQUE TO SOCIETY

One striking aspect of the mosque is the particular place, or in some cases the absence of place, reserved for women. The interior of the mosque is usually divided into two very distinct spaces, reflecting the gendered nature of Muslim society. The religious dimension of *ṣalāh* and devotion to God need not be evaluated through the gendered division of the mosque. Men and women do not occupy different positions in relation to God. However, the spatial distinctions for men and women in the mosque denote different socialization for Muslim men and women. Most contemporary Muslims would insist that such a division did not necessarily imply that women were inferior to men. Other observers, however, take this to be a reflection of the 'inherent subordination to men in the Islamic tradition' (Tapper 1990: 249). The truth lies somewhere between the external criticisms and the internal justifications. The gendered construction of Muslim space is not fixed, and the position of women is continuously changing, but some of the complexities lie deep in religious texts, interpretations and social expectations.

In conformity with the following Prophetic statement, men and women take on different positions in the mosque: 'The best of rows for men are in the front and the worst at the back; and the best of rows for women are in the back and the worst in the front' (Ṣiddīqī 1976: I, 239). The middle rows are usually reserved for children. Hence, one can visualize men and women occupying their respective places in the mosque from two very different, but equally honourable, places. To a certain extent, this statement by itself inscribes a spatial complementarity, in that there are two different but meritorious places for men and women. The front or the first rows do not necessarily have an inherently higher value than the others. The first is only relatively meritorious, since it only applies to men, and the same can be said for women at the back. It is this sense of symmetry and complementarity which many Muslims espouse when they insist on the equitable relations between men and women inside the mosque, and by extension in Islam.

Unfortunately, one needs to go beyond one statement, well-known and popular though it may be, to appreciate the gendered nature of Islamic space. The ideal position espoused in the Prophetic statement needs to be reconsidered in the light of other statements attributed to him, as well as in the light of the actual practice of Muslims since then.

Numerous statements of the Prophet have been handed down, and the usual practice in Islam is to put them all together before making a judgement on an issue. Ordinarily, Muslim scholars try to find some way of reconciling contrasting statements, and read them in such a way that they reinforce each other. A similar reading will be attempted here, but with the assumption that the initial statement quoted above ought to be taken as the norm. In particular, the spatial complementarity suggested in the statement would be our starting point for reading two other statements concerning the same issue. It is also reported that the Prophet said: 'The first row is like the row of angels. If you knew its merit, you would be competing for it.' And yet in another statement related by 'Ā'ishah, the wife of the Prophet, the Prophet said: 'God and the angels send salutation on those on the right-hand side of the rows' (Ibn Qudāmah 1968: II, 161). The second Prophetic statement, extolling the front rows in an absolute sense, is silent about the equally meritorious back rows for women. Taken with a touch of hermeneutic suspicion, however, it is justifiable to regard it as a statement excluding the merit of the back rows, particularly those occupied by women. Such a reading can only be justified, though, if the first Prophetic statement is forgotten or ignored. And this, as many contemporary Muslim women are arguing, is precisely what has happened in Islamic scholarship. Since such scholarship has been almost the exclusive preserve of men, it is not surprising to see how a statement extolling the virtues of the front row is conspicuously silent on the merits of the back row. While the first statement imprints a complementarity of space, perhaps even its equality, the second negates the meritorious back rows of women by its omission and silence on the rows reserved by women.

In the light of these competing conceptualizations, the third statement from the Prophet is not fortuitously narrated by 'Ā'ishah, the favourite wife of the Prophet, who has been regarded as the champion of the rights of women in early Islam. Especially after the Prophet's death, she seems to have argued against the circulation of Prophetic statements which tried to put women 'in their place'. In this case, then, the statement may not simply be an innocent remark about the right-hand rows in a mosque. The political impact of this *ḥadīth* becomes particularly sharp in the light of the first and second *ḥadīths*. The first established the mosque as a symmetrical space, the second privileged the front, while 'Ā'ishah's narration reaffirmed the first with dramatic textual power. By extolling the virtues of the right-hand rows, 'Ā'ishah's statement was not simply asking Muslims to fill the mosque from the right side. This has been the conventional meaning attributed to the statement. Rather, in the light of the politics of gendered space of a mosque, the eminence of the right-hand rows spreads the merit through both the front and the back rows. While the second *ḥadīth* privileges the front, the third includes the back rows in merit.

A brief note on the life of ʻĀ'ishah (d. 678) would place this discussion in perspective. She was born in Mecca and married the Prophet at a very young age. It seems that like his other marriages, this one was also initially contracted for 'political' purposes. The marriage between the Prophet and ʻĀ'ishah was in fact suggested by another woman, Khawlah bt. al-Ḥakam, in order to strengthen the ties between Muhammad and one of his closest friends. ʻĀ'ishah was the daughter of Abū Bakr and a close associate of the Prophet. The marriage grew deep and affectionate but, like all marriages, was severely tested. In one such case, ʻĀ'ishah had accompanied the Prophet on a military expedition, but on the return journey she was left behind when she lingered to look for a lost necklace. The rest of the group proceeded to Medina without her. One of the Prophet's Companions then escorted her back to Medina, an incident which generated great suspicion and rumour. ʻĀ'ishah, however, stood her ground until revelation from Gabriel cleared her name. When the Prophet died, ʻĀ'ishah was only eighteen but she subsequently played a significant political and intellectual role in early Islam. Her political role came to a head when the third caliph ʻUthmān was assassinated in his home. She went to Mecca and, together with some prominent Companions of the Prophet, led a campaign to avenge the caliph's death. The expedition resulted in a battle with the next caliph, ʻAlī, and eventually led to ʻĀ'ishah giving up political activity.

However, she continued to act as an outspoken teacher, who seemed to be alert to the tendencies to relegate women to secondary status. A modern Muslim feminist from Morocco, Fatimah Mernissi, has studied some of her juridical views, and relates the following classic and typical riposte. ʻĀ'ishah heard the following statement attributed to the Prophet: 'The dog, the ass and the woman interrupt prayer if they pass in front of the believer, interposing themselves between him and the *qiblah* (the direction of prayer).' She immediately replied: 'You compare us now to asses and dogs. In the name of God, I have seen the Prophet saying prayers while I was there, lying between him and the *qiblah*. And in order not to disturb him I did not move' (Mernissi 1991: 64, 70). This statement seems to confirm a pattern in 'Ā'ishah's regard for women's welfare, and clearly illustrates how one may understand her statement concerning the rows in a mosque. It is not difficult to imagine that the statement was a powerful gesture in the debate as to where women should sit in a mosque.

Unfortunately, the actual practice of Muslims in relation to gender has been even more one-sided than my analysis of Prophetic statements and 'Ā'ishah's responses would suggest. Thus, in spite of these statements, women have been progressively excluded from the mosques. The legal schools, in particular, do not regard Friday and congregational prayer incumbent upon Muslim women. The following quotation from Ibn Qudāmah, a great twelfth-century Ḥanbalī jurist, is extremely revealing for what it says about women attending Friday service in particular, and by implication their role in society in subsequent jurisprudence. According to Ibn Qudāmah, women may attend the Friday service, but they are not required to do so. His reasoning reveals his particular conception of Friday worship and the place of women therein. Women ought not attend 'because Friday service gathers together men and the woman is not part of the assembly of men. Nevertheless, her Friday prayer is valid because she is allowed to join the congregation (*jamā'ah*) as the women used to pray with the Prophet in congregation' (Ibn Qudāmah 1968: II, 243). Compared to other Sunni legal schools, the Ḥanbalī school is particularly open to admitting women to mosques. More often, women are positively discouraged from attending Friday service; many mosques will not even allow women into the building. Nevertheless, Ibn Qudāmah's statement reveals a clear justification for the exclusion of women from Friday congregational worship as a matter of principle. As a symbol and expression of the assembly of men, the Friday service could 'naturally' exclude women. At the same time, the statement reveals a rupture between this justification and the practice of the Prophet, in which women used to be part of the congregation. The jurist makes a concession to cover this breach by stating that the woman's Friday worship is valid. The 'validity' is a legal concession that cannot cover up the crack between how women attended the Friday service, an assembly of men, during the time of the Prophet, and how they were granted secondary status in jurisprudence. Certainly, we have moved far away from the first *ḥadīth* with which I had opened the discussion, which insisted on equality and complementarity. And, as I have noted, Ibn Qudāmah reveals a fairly 'liberal' approach to women in the mosque in a period when women were being excluded from the mosque altogether.

In the twentieth century, the doors of the mosque are being reopened for women. In some, women are reoccupying the rear of the mosque, while in others provision is made in special places completely cut off from the men. In both cases, however, the dominant ethos concerning gender is that expressed by Ibn Qudāmah. Women are silent and marginalized and, in the view of many, do not really need to be inside the mosque at all. A few mosques, however, are beginning to reconsider the spatial dynamics of the building and are dividing the mosque lengthways, one side for men and the other for women. This reorganization of space sometimes meets with fierce opposition from Muslims who insist that women and men should be organized in the mosque according to the literal statement of the Prophet. In this regard, the Prophetic statement is invoked as an imposition of a formal and literal organization wherein women do not feature too significantly, and not as a symbolic statement of its time. The irony of the modern debate is that opposition to change mostly comes from those who deny women any place in the mosque. Those who insist that women may only occupy the rear of the mosque do not make any provision for them. If they attend at all, they are expected to sit in one corner or a basement, anywhere where their ritual exclusion reflects and symbolizes their social marginalization.

The debate on Islamic space signifies the difficulty of reconciling the religious and social place of women in Islam. There is general agreement that women have the same religious and spiritual responsibilities and privileges as men within the religious tradition. On the other hand, society is deeply divided along public/private and male/female axes. Accordingly, women's primary responsibility and preserve is the home, while men move freely in public places. Thus, to take another example, a woman's testimony in matters of business transactions is worth half that of a man: 'let two witnesses among men testify to the document; if there are no two men, then one man and two women among the witnesses with whom you are happy, so that when one errs, the other may remind her' (Qur'ān 2:282). This verse has vexed many contemporary Muslim women scholars, but it at least underlines the fact that women are not expected to engage in business to the same extent as men. Whether it implies that this should always be the case is a matter hotly debated among Muslims.

The gendered division of Muslim society has also led to some differences between women's religious practices and those of men. Since orthodoxy is usually a measure of public religious belief and practice, women's religious practices have been relatively less affected and perhaps less hindered by dogma and creed. Nancy Tapper's study of women's religious practices in Turkey has shown this sharp contrast in the observance of Mevlūd, the Turkish celebration of the birthday of the Prophet. In Turkey, the customary celebration has not been eliminated by the *bid'ah* charges, but it has been transformed. Where the festivals once celebrated and symbolized fertility and individual salvation, they now emphasize 'temporal life, sobriety and social morality' as defined by official Turkish Islam. According to Nancy Tapper's ethnography, moreover, women's celebrations of the Mevlūd were relatively unaffected by these political influences compared to those of men. Thus, women, in contrast with men

> fulfil a more dramatic function. In their services, which almost always occur in the context of death, women create and confirm the promise of individual salvation which is offered to all Muslims. The women's Mevlūds do this by exalting childbirth and using an ideal of motherhood to establish an intimate link between the Mevlūd participants and the Prophet Muhammad.
>
> (Tapper and Tapper 1987: 84)

This pattern of men and women living in complementary worlds is found in other Muslim contexts as well. By itself, it may be said that the different approach to Islam, women's Islam, may be entrenching women's marginalized social position (Tapper 1990).

In fact, the place of women in religion in general, and in Islam in particular, has been the subject of intense research. Tapper's study in Turkey has pointed to the complimentary and unequal worlds inhabited by men and women. Others have found some surprising evidence of women asserting themselves in a male-dominated world. This assertion has been subtle but, in its cultural context, empowering. As a demonstration of this, I introduce the analysis of a Swahili poem suggested by Anne Biersteker (1991). This poem, which belongs to the Utenzi collection of East Africa, was composed by the wife of a religious leader in the 1850s. The Utendi wa Mwana Kupona is usually read to a young woman by her grandmother on the night before she is married. On the surface, the poem seems to be a classic case of women reinforcing the dominant male-centred cosmology. The young girl's religious duties towards God, the Prophet and her parents are enmeshed with a dutiful and doting responsibility towards her husband:

> Of God and His Prophet
> father and mother you know
> and the fifth is of your husband
> often it has been repeated

Biersteker, however, suggest that a second reading of the poem reveals its deeply subversive nature. The young girl is not simply taught how to cope with the male world, she is also taught how to prosper in it. Principally, she is encouraged to make use of the power of speech:

> You should have good manners and a skilled tongue
> so that you are a loved person wherever you enter
> Make yourself affable through words which are not guileful
> nor should you be malicious such that people will hate you

Speech is to be used in relation to her husband in the most skilful of ways:

> You should praise your husband
> So his reputation spreads
> But you should not insist of him
> That which he cannot produce

This piece shows how the young woman can control her relationship. Whilst she is expected to praise the qualities of her husband, she must control herself and thus determine what others think of him. A careful and skilful use of words will reverse the dominant social positions in society:

> If he gets sleepy, do not leave him
> or mention it by a cry
> but stay right there, don't get up
> When he rouses he will find you
> When he rouses you shouldn't rest
> Provide him with sustenance
> Satisfy him and care for his body
> Massage him, and bathe him

From one perspective, it appears that the poem is teaching subservience. On another reading, however, it reflects the subtle power of a woman coping and thriving in a male-dominated society. Caring for a dominant person turns that person into a child, as the poem in fact states: 'Care for him like a child who does not know how to speak' (Biersteker 1991). The Swahili poem, then, is one example through which one can appreciate the particular role played by Muslim women in male-dominated societies. It is not simply a case of women cowering under the threat of male abuse.

The particular place of women in modern Islamic societies is open to change, and it is difficult to say how relations may change. What is true, however, is the fact that women's practices in Islam may and do hold much significance for understanding Islam in context. And, as I believe, they offer much to men who care to listen and take note.

AESTHETICS

I have mentioned earlier that jurists were at pains to point out that decoration should be avoided inside a mosque. And truly, most mosques have been humble buildings providing a demarcated space for worship; no more and no less. This is often overlooked when we think of the grand mosques that grace so many cities and towns where Muslims live. The following section, though, will deal precisely with the art exhibited in both humble and grand mosques. Muslims with financial means, usually rulers and wealthy merchants, have spent generously to decorate mosques with some of the most exquisite calligraphy and arabesque. Using space and form, they have been able to project the fundamental beliefs and values of Islam in art forms. To a lesser extent, the artistic expression in these grand mosques is reflected, albeit less ostentatiously, in humbler mosques. And so it is to an appreciation of art in mosques and elsewhere that I wish to turn in this section.

Islamic art includes a great variety of forms, of which mosque architecture represents only one dimension. The recitation of the Qur'ān and the calligraphic shaping of letters into exquisite forms are also key forms of art. One should add to that the calligraphic decoration of the walls of mosques and palaces, and sometimes also village homes. Arabesque, the use of stylized plants and geometric designs, sometimes by themselves but often together with imbedded calligraphy, is another form of Islamic decoration. Music, yet another form of art, has already been discussed in Chapter 1 of this work. Last, and by no means the least, one must also include the prayer carpet, a medium that brings together the principal features of Islamic art in a concentrated form.

As the study of the general principles of beautification and art, aesthetics is a modern development. Consequently, there is great debate among scholars as to the significance and meaning of the artistic tradition in the world of Islam. There is some agreement that the art produced by Muslims exhibits a unity that transcends local variations. By implication, therefore, there should be some underlying foundational philosophy that produces this art. However, this is where disagreement still exists. The artists of early Islamic culture have not left much by way of theories or philosophies of art. In their absence, suggestions of theories abound. In this section, I wish to introduce the theories of two of the leading scholars of Islam. I include these, and not others, because they are insider statements of the religious value and location of the art. Seyyed Hossein Nasr approaches Islamic art from the perspective of the mystic who produced the art; while Ismā'īl and Lois Lamyā' al Fārūqī propose a theory of art which focuses on the appreciation of its visual and sound effects. Nasr suggests that it is the inner spirit of the human artist that produced art; the al Fārūqīs suggest how art may be viewed and appreciated.

Nasr insists that we should approach Islamic art from the religion's inner dimensions, the mystical tradition called Sufism. The variety of Islamic art, reflecting the diversity of geographical and cultural groups, should not be confused with its essence, or with the appreciation of beauty in Islam. The latter is fundamentally a deeply religious and pietistic exercise. As Nasr so eloquently says, 'the origins of Islamic art must be sought in the inner realities of the Qur'ān which are also the principle realities of the cosmos and the spiritual realities of the Prophetic substance from which flows the Muhammadan grace (*al-barakah al-muhammadiyyah*)' (Nasr 1990: 6). Nasr goes on to argue that the unity that binds Islamic art should be sufficient argument against scholars of Islamic art who dare to limit it to local, social and historical accidents. The thread that runs through Islam's art, whether in calligraphy on a mosque wall, recitation of the Qur'ān, or an exquisite carpet, unmistakably points to its unity. And in that unity lies the source of Islamic art.

Nasr goes further, asserting that the art of Islam is principally a manifestation of the unity of God. The use of the different media of art produces a striking visual image of the primary belief in Islam, which is that there is no god but the God. Again, to quote Nasr on this issue:

> Islamic art is the result of the manifestation of Unity upon the plane of multiplicity. It reflects in a blinding manner the unity of the Divine principle, the dependence of all multiplicity upon the One, the ephemerality of the world and the positive qualities of cosmic existence or creation about which God asserts in the Qur'ān, 'Our Lord! Thou hast not created this in vain.'
>
> (Nasr 1990: 7)

Art, therefore, is a projection of the fundamental belief in Islam. This brings us directly to the production and the producers of Islamic art. Since Islamic art is a reflection of the unity of God, its source can only be God:

> Those who have created objects of Islamic art over the ages have done so either by being able to gain a vision of that archetypal world, thanks to the means available by the Islamic revelation and specifically the Muhammadan *barakah*, or have been instructed by those who have had such a vision.
>
> (Nasr 1990: 7)

Thus, the inspiration of Islamic art was not simply a reflection of 'individualistic inspiration or creativity' (Nasr 1990: 7). Art could only be called Islamic if it was directly connected with the primary sources of inspiration in Islam, which are God and the Prophet Muhammad. For example, calligraphy was produced by saints who regarded themselves as the pen in the hand of God (Nasr 1990: 24). Since the Prophet Muhammad was the agent through which revelation was effected, art also seeks to reconnect with the Divine through his blessing (*barakah*).

This was possible through a contemplation of the Qur'ān, the Prophet, or nature, which were all ultimately reflections of the sacred texts of God. In this interpretation of Islamic art, the architecture of the mosque takes on a cosmic dimension. Taking the statement of the Prophet that the entire earth was made a mosque for worship, Nasr developed an intricate exposition of the resanctification of nature:

> the root of the sacred architecture of Islam is to be found in this re-sanctification of nature in relation to man seen as the primordial being who remains aware of his inner nexus both to the One and to His

> creation, as well as subsequent relationships between architecture and the Islamic cosmos with its cosmological laws and principles described so majestically in the Quran and elucidated and elaborated by generations of sages throughout the history of Islam.
>
> (Nasr 1990: 40)

Humankind, nature and God are intrinsically related to each other through Islamic worship. The believer's worship within nature (the mosque par excellence) captures his or her relationship both to God and to nature as the creation of God. The mosque as an artistic expression tries to express this relationship. For Nasr, the classical domed mosque thus symbolizes the levels of creation from God down to the material world (Nasr 1990: 41). In the mosque itself, 'stillness reflects the pacifying presence of the Divine Word which echoes through it' and the 'rhythmic division of the space by means of arches and columns is the counterpart to the rhythms of cosmic existence which punctuate the phases of the life of man as well as the cosmos'. Mathematical exactness and harmony, permeating the architecture of a mosque, direct attention away from temporality and change (Nasr 1990: 47–8). In fact, all the lines of a mosque refer to the signs of God; their emptiness reflects the poverty of this world and the presence of nothing but God (Nasr 1990: 44, 47). This breathtaking interpretation of mosque architecture provides a glimpse of the creative genius of Islam which produced the legacy of Islamic art in deeply spiritual contexts.

The al Fārūqīs suggest a very different approach to understanding Islamic art. Beginning from a very non-mystical position, which does not accommodate the spiritual stance assumed by Nasr, Ismā'īl al Fārūqī and his wife Lamyā' al Fārūqī suggest another way of understanding Islamic art. Their attitude towards Islamic art represents a contemporary approach for many Muslims, who often blame Sufism for many of the problems facing Islam today. They think that aspects of Sufism, such as the total dependence on a spiritual master expected of a Sufi novice, were responsible for the ills affecting Muslim individuals and societies. In any case, this approach to Islamic art does not deal with the mystical rapture that produces Islamic art. Rather than the mystical visions of immanentism, this 'transcendence-obsessed culture, sought', says Lamyā' al Fārūqī, 'through the creation of the beautiful, to stimulate in the viewer or listener an intuition of, or an insight into, the nature of Allah . . . and of man's relation to Him' (al Fārūqī 1985: 19). On the basis of the forms and patterns of Islamic art, the al Fārūqīs propose fundamental principles governing Islamic music, painting, calligraphy and architecture.

All forms of Islamic art deliberately set out to 'disguise and transfigure nature . . . Mass, volume, depth, perspective, space, enclosure, gravity, cohesion, tension are all elements that have been aesthetically negated by the Islamic artist' (al Fārūqī 1985: 21). Thus, stylization, non-individuation and repetition in various forms of art remove any semblance of nature within art. Art cannot and does not aim to represent nature in any form. The human being is, in principle, unable to reproduce the creation of God, and he or she depicts this principled inability by stylizing plants, denying individuality to human figures, and robbing nature of depth and character. Rather like the Qur'ān, art flows continuously, produced not 'in its logically progressive thought, but in the sparks of genius which flash before us for a moment in each successive partition' (al Fārūqī 1985: 24). This continuous flow is artistically achieved by the use of arabesque, patterns produced by the combination of geometric figures, calligraphy and stylized elements. According to Lamyā' al Fārūqī, the arabesque provides the artist with an ideal medium in which to combine forms and produce a combination of patterns, endless in principle and effect.

The artist, and later the consumer, appreciates art of arabesque by following the intricate detail of one segment, absorbing it, and then passing on to another. Each segment may be deciphered for its use of a variety of forms. Sometimes it consists of geometric designs, sometimes stylized plants, at other times intricate calligraphic conventions. The artist moves within the work of art: 'As each arabesque pattern is grasped and understood, the spectator feels a launch of his spirit with his success, and he moves to the next pattern' (al Fārūqī 1985: 29). The ultimate 'launch', the artistic insight, is attained when the search proceeds from one segment to another, repeated endlessly. The search is not exhausted because one has reached the end of the canvas or melody, but because the search for the ultimate is necessarily inexhaustible. This movement from one pattern to another, one calligraphic style to another, reproduces the search for knowing God. In theology and metaphysics, one moves from one name to another. Just as the names of God, infinite in number in principle, give us a glimpse of the nature of God, the arabesque segments do the same as they simulate a search for the Ultimate inexpressible value. The Qur'ān says, 'nothing is like unto

Him', and the artistic genius of Islam used arabesque to reproduce the aesthetic equivalent of this profound statement.

The space inside the mosque provided us with an opportunity to explore how Islam defines religious and, by extension, social space. The emptiness of the mosque means that the sacred is defined through symbolic acts, political and religious. The mosque refracts the ways in which Muslims organize social and political space, but also in different ways it is also the springboard for communal and individual devotion. In Islam, moreover, space has always been highly compartmentalized as far as gender is concerned. At the end of the twentieth century, a battle rages over this, as women claim their rightful place inside mosque and in public space in general. Finally, the architecture, art and decoration of mosques provide an opportunity to appreciate Islamic aesthetics. Nasr suggested a philosophy emanating from deep mysticism, while the al Fārūqīs showed us a way of appreciating the art from an observer's point of view.

4 THE PRAYER NICHE
The inexpressible goal of Islamic devotion

The interior of the mosque is empty of any cultic materials, its space created by the performance of rituals like the *ṣalāh* and the recitation of the Qur'ān. However, in almost all mosques, one usually finds a niche (*miḥrāb*) in the front wall, a slight recess which indicates the direction of the Inviolable House (*al-bayt al-ḥarām*) in Mecca. It is this particular direction, called the *qiblah*, which all Muslims must face when turning to prayer. Some of the great mosques in Islam also feature *miḥrāb*s along the other walls of the mosque. These recesses provide opportunities for personal devotion like the recitation of the Qur'ān and *dhikr* (remembrance of God). Sometimes they are large enough for a small group to gather in one for similar religious purposes. The *miḥrāb* in the mosque provides an interesting point of departure for a discussion of the ultimate goal of Islamic worship. As it faces in the direction of Mecca, it will also be used in this chapter to explore the place and meaning of pilgrimage in Islam. This in turn will take us to a discussion of the nature of the Islamic community (*ummah*).

An intriguing feature of the *miḥrāb* and its direction, the *qiblah*, is the fact that it represents a self-effacing central point in a mosque. We approach the mosque by heeding the call to prayer, then performing ablution, entering the mosque, and finally engaging in worship. The immediate goal of these activities is standing and facing Mecca, a direction indicated by the *miḥrāb*. From this perspective, the *miḥrāb* represents the spatial end-point of a movement towards a particular direction. When we arrive at the *miḥrāb*, however, we find that it points away from the mosque, indicating that the spiritual journey is not over.

Thus the mosque is not an end-point, but a fundamental starting-point for a journey that must go beyond the here and now. The al Fārūqīs, whose insights were discussed in the last chapter, pointed out the ways in which this ceaseless, continuous journey expresses the inexpressible in Islamic art. The act of going to a mosque recreates the same aesthetic journey in a daily ritual. Like the appreciation of a piece of Islamic art which seeks to induce the inexpressibility of ultimate value in Islam, the goal of worship cannot reside inside the confines of a mosque, however expansive and profound that might seem. Certainly, the journey to God must have a station, a goal on the religious quest which must be transcended if one is to journey to the Absolute. In this case the mosque is the station, but it must also be the starting point for a further, higher station. The *miḥrāb* in the mosque represents a journey of many stations. The Sufis seem to have expressed this well when they spoke of stations (*maqāmāt*) on a journey to God. Their stations corresponded to attitudes and states of being: fear, hope, love, etc. Like the Sufi's evolution through pyschological states, the *miḥrāb* indicates that the journey to God is not a long, continuous one, but consists of continually unfolding stages. This metaphor has profound implications for how one knows and approaches God.

HOW DO WE KNOW?

The significance of the *miḥrāb* as a symbol of a stage on the journey to God leads us to some of the fundamental questions raised in Islamic theology during the early history of Islam, which continue to be raised in our times. These questions concern the human ability to know in general, and to know God and human obligations in particular. How do we know God? Can we rely on revelation in the form of scripture? How about history and the natural world? Does reason play a role in understanding God? And how do we know our obligations towards God in particular, and towards the people and creatures of the world in general? These are some of the fundamental epistemological questions posed in early Islamic thought.

The growing community faced new challenges and sought new answers to questions as they arose within the new experiences that confronted Muslims. Thus, for example, theologians asked what was meant in the Qur'ānic verses which referred to the 'hand' of God or the 'throne' on which he sat. In addition to these classical questions of theology and the theory of knowledge, theologians also probed the definition of a believer. Did the term refer to someone who professed faith, or only someone who lived a perfect life of devotion? Some of these questions were as much political as religious questions. Since the political ruler in the Islamic order was a Muslim, the question of defining a Muslim was directly related to the issue of the status of sinful and exploiting rulers. By way of introduction to this vast and intricate subject, I will briefly look at the vexed question of defining a believer. As the intensity of revelation passed over and the religion began to spread, the questions of definition and structures came to the fore, although this does not mean that they were theoretical issues, to be dealt with at leisure. Such theological questions affected critical aspects of early Islamic life, unlocking fundamental questions: What are the tools and resources for understanding the nature of God? How do we know the correct procedure for worship and prayer? And on what basis do we establish the perfect social and political order? The various theological schools in Islam posited unique answers to these questions.

One of the first issues in post-Prophetic Islamic thought concerned the status of a sinful believer. Three positions have usually been identified on this topic, but I would like to add a fourth. The first position is that of the extremist Kharijites, who demanded absolute commitment from all Muslims and declared that those who deviated from the fundamental pillars of Islam became unbelievers. Initially part of ʿAlī's army against Muʿāwiyah, they deserted him when he decided to refer the matter to arbitration, deciding then that ʿAlī had chosen to disobey God by negotiating with a renegade like Muʿāwiyah. In fact, one of their members assassinated ʿAlī for this infraction! The Kharijites went on to lead numerous rebellions against the authority of the Umayyad caliphate, charging that the caliphs were not worthy of allegiance because of their iniquity and repression. Theirs was an uncompromising position on matters of faith and practice which demanded that Muslims, and especially rulers, be perfect. In a most radical sense, they believed that everybody ought to practise what they preached. This uncompromising position may be linked to a literal understanding of the Qur'ān, which repeatedly urges believers to 'believe and do good deeds'. 'O people who believe', charged a prominent verse in the Qur'ān, 'why do you say that which you do not do? It is a grave matter in the eyes of God that you say that which you do not do' (Qur'ān 61:2–3). In contrast to its religious inspiration, the political implication of this position was equally clear. It meant that all believers were completely equal, that rulers were fully accountable to the members of the group.

From a theological point of view, the Kharijites were opposed by a moderate group, the Murji'ites, who believed that deciding the status of a believer ought to be postponed for God's judgement on the Last Day. Individual believers were not permitted to judge the value and belief of another person on the basis of outward actions. Belief and actions did not necessarily correspond at all times. On the one hand, this was a clearly more reasonable way of understanding religious disputes, as far as ordinary relations among members of a public community are concerned. Like their opponents, they too could argue that the verses in the Qur'ān implored Muslims to match faith and deeds. However, this could not be taken to imply that a political or social order ought to be founded on the basis of such appeals. This theological position was also championed by those in a particular political relation with the state. It represented the theological position of those who chose to stay out of the early civil conflict among Muslims. Consequently, a theological position that urged Muslims not to judge others by their deeds was opportune for autocratic rulers: like other believers, rulers too ought not to be judged by their deeds.

A third group, the Mu'tazilites, took a position midway between the two, and argued that a sinner at the moment of committing the sin was neither a believer nor a disbeliever. The Mu'tazilites also became embroiled in political struggles when they later urged caliphs to impose their doctrines on the religious elite. A fourth group, although not usually regarded as a theological school, must also be included when we evaluate religious responses in early Islam. Unlike the groups mentioned so far, Sufis preferred to measure the religious status of an individual by the degree of awe, reverence and love within the individual, and not as something exhibited by outward acts.

The political origins of these differences were soon forgotten as they ramified into theological branches and offshoots. The political issues were never completely submerged, but the groups developed into the fully-fledged religious tendencies that I now explore, to give the reader a general view of theology in Islam. The Kharijites became a fringe group that did not survive the first dynasty of Islam as a serious challenge to Islamic political order. In recent history, however, they have inspired many a revolutionary to fight against modern forms of oppression. Their philosophy of action and revolution has been attractive to the Muslim community even though the Kharijite name is not readily invoked. On the other hand, the Sunnis evolved from the Murji'ites of early Islam. In religious terms, they developed a position that argued that knowledge of God, Islamic legal obligations, and even history, could only be possible with the aid of revelation. The latter mainly referred to the Qur'ān, but it could also imply the *sunnah* of the Prophet Muhammad conveyed by *ḥadīth* reports. Since the Prophet was the recipient, the expounder par excellence and model of the revelation, his behavioural pattern was also regarded as a religious norm of divine experience. All questions of religious thought must begin and end with the Qur'ān or the *ḥadīth* report, traced carefully back to the Prophet or his trusted Companions. Clearly, this was the legacy of al-Shāfi'ī, discussed earlier in this work.

In theological terms, the Sunnis may be further divided between a Ḥanbalī position in reference to Aḥmad b. Ḥanbal, and an Ash'arī one in reference to Abū 'l-Ḥasan 'Alī b. Ismā'īl al-Ash'arī (d. 935). The Ḥanbalīs insisted that all forms of revelation should be accepted, and believed in their literal import without any kind of rationalization. This was the position popularized in the phrase *bilā kayf* (literally, 'without asking how'). Accordingly, theological questions, particularly those pertaining to knowledge of the unseen, must be accepted as a matter of faith. Knowledge of God, his name and attributes, the nature of humanity, and other fundamental questions of human existence, should be sought from the Qur'ān and the *sunnah* understood in their literal import. The Ash'arī position also began and ended with the Qur'ān and the *ḥadīth*, but it tried to rationalize the meaning of the terms they used. Thus, for example, the Ḥanbalīs simply accepted the fact, without asking how, of God's 'hand' because it appeared in the Qur'ān. The Ash'arīs argued that such a term implied his authority. The reality of God's hand, if understood only in its literal meaning, would lead to anthropomorphism, which is rejected by the belief in God's transcendence. In general, the Ash'arī position stood midway between the literal position of the Ḥanbalīs and the rational position of the Mu'tazilites. In fact, the founder of the school, al-Ash'arī, was first a Mu'tazilite before he recanted and developed a synthesis between the two antagonistic positions. The Ash'arīs posited a linguistic solution that satisfied the demands of Qur'ānic terminology and reason: 'It [the attribute] is not he [God] nor other than him' (*lā huwa huwa wa lā huwa ghayruh*) is the well-known compromise that tries to assert the reality of attributes as attested in scripture and rational speculation, whilst denying that they constitute realities apart from God. Both the Ash'arī and Ḥanbalī positions are popular among most contemporary Sunni groups.

The epistemological foundation of both the Ḥanbalīs and the Ash'arīs on the literal import of texts implied a particular dimension of the religious quest. In some senses, this celebration of the text has greater impact in religious practice than in theology. If we think again about the *miḥrāb* and its particular religious orientation, it is an approach that tends to place all emphasis on following in the footsteps of the Prophet Muhammad and his Companions in as wide a sense as possible. In addition to the values taught by the Prophet, salvation also lies in eating like him, walking and even greeting like him. These symbols, meticulously followed and recalled, become the means to a virtuous and religious life. The major emphasis is an attempt to revive and recall the behavioural model established by the Prophet. One must follow the *ḥadīth* attributed to the Prophet himself which says: 'Whoever revives one of my *sunnah*s [behavioural norms] which has become extinct after me, he will have the reward of all those who follow it without diminishing their rewards' (Ibn Mājah n. d.: Ch. 15, no. 209/211). This form of religious quest can take on an extremely 'primitive', back-to-basics orientation, and may be compared with the attitudes of many in the modern world who choose a lifestyle that privileges the natural, simple and austere. Many Muslims, emulating the Prophet's lifestyle, wear white clothes, eat sitting on the ground and generally shun ostentation. Following the example of the Prophet thus generates a degree of contentment and poise which is admirable and fulfilling. However, it should be noted that such a *sunnah* ethic is not driven by naturalism as such. The focus lies not in the value of rustic romanticism, but in the principle of emulation. Therefore, in some cases, the austere and simple example of the Prophet Muhammad can be juxtaposed with extreme symbols of technological innovation. Simple white robes, for example, the epitome of grace and austerity, can and are sometimes combined with the most recent models of cellular phones.

One of the principal contributions of Sunni legal and theological thinking, this path to God can be seen in other Muslim groups as well. The Shi'ites, in principle, did not share the political quietism of the Sunnis of early Islam. Unlike the Sunnis, they did not in principle accept the authority of caliphs who were not descendents of 'Alī, the cousin and son-in-law of the Prophet, and Fāṭimah, the daughter of the Prophet. In practice, however, mainstream Shi'ites accepted political authority as a lesser of two evils. This acquiescent position has been overshadowed by recent political events in which Shi'ism has been identified with radical political uprisings. From a religious perspective, if we substitute for the Imāms (descendents of the Prophet Muhammad) in Shi'ism the Companions of the Prophet in Sunnism, we find a similar passion for the forms of religious life. One also finds the same valuing of austerity and simplicity in Shi'ite religious life that is generated within Sunnism. In Shi'ism, however, it is motivated by a commitment to follow the example both of the Prophet Muhammad and of the Imāms: 'Since the Prophet and, for the Shi'is, the Imams were sinless and infallible, their words and deeds are a guide and model for all to follow' (Momen 1985: 173). And thus Shi'ite religious life revolves around the examples established by the Prophetic family from Muhammad to 'Alī, Fāṭimah, her two sons, Ḥasan and Ḥusayn, and then the other Imāms. It should not be forgotten, of course, that in the early centuries of Islam, the Imāms were highly regarded as scholars and pietists among Sunnis as well, although Sunnis did not regard them as the divinely appointed exemplars as the Shi'ites did. In Sunni thinking, the descendents of the Prophet were part of a whole array of pious followers of the Prophet who preserved the standards of Islamic life and thought.

Ja'far al-Ṣādiq, the sixth Imām of the Twelver Shi'ites, is highly regarded for establishing a system of jurisprudence comparable to that of the Sunni schools discussed earlier. He was born in Medina and his mother, Umm Farwā, was the great-granddaughter of Abū Bakr. This in itself suggests that, among the early scholars at least, the divisions between the various tendencies were not as clearly drawn as later histories tend to suggest. Ja'far al-Ṣādiq was highly regarded by all scholars for his knowledge of jurisprudence and *ḥadīth*, and is credited with laying the foundation of Shi'ite understanding of law and religious obligations. In political terms, however, he supported the non-militant Shi'ites, and in fact he refused to support the revolt of Muḥammad al-Nafs al-Zakiyyah (d. 762–3) which his Sunni contemporaries Abū Ḥanīfah and Mālik b. Anas endorsed in one way or another. However, Ja'far al-Ṣādiq was recognized as a potentially more powerful symbol of a possible Shi'ite rebellion, and was reportedly poisoned on the orders of the Abbasid Caliph al-Manṣūr in 765.

In contrast with the Sunnis and the Shi'ites, the Mu'tazilites espoused rational speculation as the first source of religious knowledge and inspiration. The following statement of Qāḍī 'Abd al-Jabbār

(d. 1024) encapsulates the central role of reason in the search to know God:

> If it is asked: What is the first duty that God imposes upon you? Say to him: speculative reasoning which leads to knowledge of God, because he is not known intuitively nor by the senses . . . then if it is asked: why did speculative reasoning become the first of the duties? say to him: Because the rest of the stipulates of revelation concerning what we should say and do are not good until after there is knowledge of God. Do you not see that it is no good for us to pray without knowing to whom we are to pray?
>
> (Martin et al. 1997: 90)

This is a remarkable statement for many Muslims who would place belief in God as the first duty. Logically, it states that rational inquiry ought to be the starting point of the religious quest. The place of reason and rational inquiry (*naẓar*) in Mu'tazilite theology has far-reaching ramifications for understanding the Qur'ān, theology and religious obligations. The Qur'an, Mu'tazilites argued, itself appealed to human reason as the first source of argument for the existence of God. It urges readers to think and reflect about nature, history and existence:

> And among his signs is the creation of the heavens and the earth and the plurality of your languages and colours. Most surely in these are signs for the knowledgable.
>
> (Qur'ān 30:22).

The terms *tafakkur* (thinking), *tadabbur* (reflection) and *'aql* (reason) are strewn throughout the Qur'ān, and the Mu'tazilites took this to establish the primacy of reason in Islam. This approach is also followed in the understanding of history in general, and early Islam in particular. In contrast to Sunnis, the Mu'tazilites believed that a historical report traced through reliable narrators should be subject to rational inquiry and evaluation, and should not be accepted at face value only on the basis of a chain of narrators. The Mu'tazilite position can be contrasted with the following unequivocal statement from al-Ṭabarī (d. 923), one of the great early historians in Islam, who thrived on collecting and arranging reports. The statement reveals his insistence that history is not open to rational speculation:

> Let the reader know that the reports (*akhbār*) that have been related here, and the reports that we have relied upon, have for the most part not been

> deduced by the proofs of the intellect, nor have they been carefully evaluated. Knowledge connected with the happenings of the past, and that which is related to information on historical persons, cannot be attained except from those who have witnessed it, and who have lived in that period. This knowledge of the past can then be traced to the reports of the reporters without any help from the intellectual and rational faculties.
>
> (al-Ṭabarī 1879–1901: I, 6–7).

The Muʿtazilites would disagree with this statement in so far as rational inquiry was suspended in the face of a report from the past. In their view, the report by itself could not produce certainty unless subject to rational scrutiny. On the basis of such reasoning, they argued that Islam was founded on five fundamental pillars: the unity of God; divine justice; the promise and threat of God; the intermediate position of a sinner; and commanding good and prohibiting evil. Each of these fundamentals was both rationally justifiable and accorded with the teachings of the Qur'ān and the Prophet Muhammad.

The Shiʿites, it should be mentioned at this juncture, shared important doctrines with the Muʿtazilites, particularly the doctrine of divine justice and the principle of commanding the good and forbidding evil (Momen 1985: 177, 180). Reason played a greater role in Shiʿite jurisprudence. In opposition to the use of analogical reasoning (*qiyās*) among the Sunnis, Shiʿite jurisprudence insisted on the use of reason to expand Islamic law. We may recall here the desire of al-Shāfiʿī to control and limit the forms of Islamic practice by the use of analogy. The Shiʿites rejected analogy and continued to develop rational modes of applying Islamic law. Muʿtazilism, then, had a profound impact on the development of Shiʿite conceptualization. It can be argued that when Muʿtazilism was discredited in the ninth and tenth centuries (as we shall see in the next chapter) some of its teachings became influential in other religious schools, and particularly Shiʿism.

The rational emphasis of the Muʿtazilites has found much favour with Muslim modernists of the nineteenth and twentieth centuries. From the nineteenth century, intellectuals like Muhammad ʿAbduh (d. 1906), Fazlur Rahmān (d. 1988) and Harun Nasution, of Egypt, Pakistan and Indonesia respectively, argued for a return to rational inquiry in Muslim communities. Reason and rational inquiry, they believed, would uplift Muslim societies and rid them of illiteracy, obscurantism and under-development. While the Muʿtazilites were mainly concerned with the rational discovery of God, their modern counterparts concerned themselves with the importance of development in the aftermath of colonialism. They believed that the total reliance on reports and precedents from tradition prevented Muslims from realizing the true values of Islam. Properly understood, Islam opened up great possibilities for Muslim societies in the twentieth century. Unlike the Mu'tazilites, most of the contemporary proponents of Mu'tazilite thought are not directly concerned with reason as a means to understand or experience God. As Richard Martin has so aptly put it:

> Mu'tazilism has come to serve not so much as doctrinal resource for constructing particular arguments against contemporary forms of traditionalism, but, rather, as a symbol of the will to be Islamic in a modern, pluralist world in which Muslims share social and political space with other confessional communities, as well as with secularism.
>
> (Martin et al. 1997: 220)

Reason, not blind faith, must guide the construction of communities. Certainly, there were social and political implications of early Mu'tazilite thought as well, but the preoccupation with social development and political liberalism is a reflection of the modern context of the debate.

A discussion of the Mu'tazilite position must be supplemented by a brief look at the philosophical approach within early Islamic history. In fact, some philosophers thought that Mu'tazilite theologians were only dabbling with reason and rationality. Ibn Rushd (1126–98) called this approach a dialectical, argumentative (*jadalī*) approach which must be contrasted with the purely demonstrative (*burhānī*) approach of the philosopher. Ibn Rushd, moreover, argued that the differences among individuals in apprehending God were related to their inherently different natures:

> The nature of people differs as to how they believe. Some believe only with demonstrative proof (*burhān*); others with argumentative reasoning because they cannot do better; and others on the basis of rhetorical statements because they too cannot do any better.
>
> (Ibn Rushd n. d.: 31)

In this regard, Islamic philosophers were unashamedly elitist: some people, by their intellectual prowess, were destined to search for truth by employing universal principles. Others could not, and should not, be allowed to dabble in such dangerous pursuits. Islamic philosophy was self-consciously a search for truth in the legacy of the great Greek thinkers. From its beginning with al-Kindī (d. 866), it argued that philosophy should not be confined to cultural boundaries:

> If the law (*shar'*) is true and appeals to reason (*naẓar*) in reaching truth, then, dear Muslims, we must know with certainty that demonstrative reasoning cannot lead us contrary to what is in the law. Truth does not contradict truth, but agrees and confirms it.
>
> (Ibn Rushd n. d.: 31)

The Muslim philosophers may be divided into broad schools. The first, represented principally by Ibn Sīnā (d. 1037) was a Neoplatonic approach which eventually merged with philosophical Sufism; while the second, best articulated by Ibn Rushd, represented the Aristotelian tradition. Both, however, tried to understand the key religious concepts in Islam like prophecy and the ideal state (the caliphate) from the perspective of reason and argument. In this regard, they continued the Greek philosophical tradition. For most of them, religion employed symbols and metaphors in order to inculcate moral values. Philosophers, who did not need to be persuaded by images and metaphors, could understand the underlying rational foundation of God, truth and felicity.

While one group insisted on the reported and visual example of the Prophet and another on the rational discovery of God, the Sufis developed yet a third approach to God. Like the two approaches discussed so far, Sufism has changed considerably over the ages, and is rich in diversity. However, if the report (*khabar* or *ḥadīth*) is the symbol of Sunnism, and rational inquiry (*'aql*) the symbol of Mu'tazilism, then experience (*dhawq*) is the dominant symbol of the Sufi *miḥrāb*. Sufis are not against reports, nor against rational inquiry as such, but they are more concerned with experiencing the divine. According to them, it is not sufficient to know God, either through reason or historical reports. Thus Margaret Smith relates an interesting statement attributed to Rābi'ah al-'Adawiyyah (d. 801) which expresses the Sufi suspicion of *ḥadīths*: 'Yes, Sufyān al-Thawrī (d. 778) would be a (good) man, if he did not love the traditions' (Smith 1928: 16). This statement should not be heeded for its historical value, but for its signification that experience was superior to learning. For the Sufi, the report or rational inquiry may provide understanding of and insight into God, but the true believer could only be satisfied with the experience of God.

Annemarie Schimmel, one of the leading expositors of Sufism in the modern world, has divided Sufism into different stages. It began with the experience of a sharp sense of awe towards God, coupled with a rejection of the world, or at least an acute awareness of its place in relation to God. It then turned to a personal, loving relationship, in which the mystic became intensely aware of his or her relationship with God. The following well-known statement from Rābiʻah resonates in the context of Sunni and Muʻtazilite thought:

> O my Lord, if I worship thee from fear of Hell, burn Me in Hell; and if I worship Thee from hope of Paradise, exclude me thence; but if I worship Thee for Thine own sake, then withhold not from me thine Eternal Beauty.
>
> (Quoted by Smith 1950: 7)

While the Muʻtazilites were insisting on the promise and threat of God that would come about on the Day of Judgement, and the Sunnis hoped for the mercy and forgiveness of God, the Sufis desired direct access to God. The Sufis then expanded this relationship. Some, like the great al-Hallāj, believed that a seeker became completely immersed in the relationship with God and extinguished in a state of self-negation (*fanā'*). Such mystical insights were only gained during overpowering moments of ecstasy, and such Sufis were regarded as the intoxicated lovers of God. Others like al-Junayd, however, insisted that this was really the first stage of a relationship with the Divine:

> My teacher (says al-Hujwīrī), who followed the doctrine of al-Junayd, used to say that intoxication is the playing-ground of children, but sobriety is the battle-field of struggle and death of men. I say, in agreement with my teacher, that the perfection of the state of the man who has been intoxicated is sobriety.
>
> (Quoted in Abdel-Kader 1962: 94)

Against the extreme lovers of God, the sober Sufis spoke of *baqā'*, or self-subsistence, in the complete presence of God. The intense personal experiences of the seekers of God was followed by a period of consolidation and rationalization. Scholars like Abū Ṭālib al-Makkī (d. 996) compiled compendiums on Sufism and biographies of the growing body of seekers. Later, in the twelfth century, this was followed by the rise of Sufi orders, which admitted a great number of people into Sufi traditions, thus ensuring that Sufism became one of the central tendencies in Islamic societies. More will be said about the orders in Chapter 5. The increase in the number of devotees did not lead to a decline in fresh insights. Sufi meditation on the relationship with God also led to a different understanding of reality. A brief discussion of one aspect of this perception will be pursued.

From an experience of God, Sufis turned to the world with a very different appreciation of nature, human society and human relationships. All of creation, nature, history and humanity, were signs (*āyāt*) of God, which could lead one back to God. Poetry was a favourite medium for expressing these insights, but Sufis also used prose. Thus, one of the greatest Sufis, Muḥyī al-Dīn ibn al-'Arabī (d. 1240), expounded his mystical insight into a comprehensive philosophy called *waḥdah al-wujūd* (unity of being). This philosophy has often been mistranslated and misunderstood as a form of pantheism, whereby everything is God and God is everything. *Waḥdah al-wujūd*, however, is a philosophy of monism in which the unity of God takes on a profound meaning. God, in this view, is not apart from his creation, and his signs exist everywhere. But the signs are not separate markers that pointed to ultimate reality. They are symbols that participate in the reality to which they refer. From this perspective of *waḥdah al-wujūd*, the verse of the Qur'an 'wheresoever you turn, there will be the face of God' (2:115) means literally just that. The face (*wajh*) in the verse does not merely point to God, but implies the very existence of God from one vantage point. In Ibn al-'Arabī's words,

> . . . this existence is His existence and that the existence of all created things, both accidents and substances, is His existence, and when the secret of one atom of the atoms is clear, the secret of all created things, both outward and inward, is clear, and you do not see in this world or the next, anything except God, for the existence of these two abodes and their name, and what they name, all of them are assuredly He.
>
> (Quoted in Smith 1950: 100)

This particular vision of reality has certainly generated much debate and dispute, but Ibn al-'Arabī has been extremely influential in Islamic philosophy and mysticism. Until the nineteenth century his vision guided other Sufis and scholars both to understand and to experience reality. His influence began to wane with the growth of political and social movements struggling against colonialism but more important for our discussion is the fact that his insights flowed from an experiential focus to knowing God.

In reflecting on the *miḥrāb* as a symbol of direction and search, we were able to explore some of the key theological and philosophical schools in Islam. The major epistemological questions in early Islam were also tinged with political overtones. However, beyond politics, they carried implications for how Muslims confronted life and its challenges. Would they rely on the verifiable report, reason, or experience? The range of possibilities highlighted the profundity of the Islamic answers to questions that continue to challenge and haunt us at the end of the twentieth century.

PILGRIMAGE

Reflections on the *miḥrāb* as a visual point of reference took us on an excursion along the possible paths that lead to God. The *miḥrāb*, as I have pointed out, also points in the direction of Mecca, particularly the Sacred House that Muslims believe was the first 'house established for humankind . . . blessed and a source of guidance' (Qur'ān 3:96). Moving now from intellectual and theological journeys to the ritual significance of the *miḥrāb*, our excursion takes us to the role and importance of pilgrimage (*ḥajj*) in Islam. Together with prayer, fasting and the alms-tax (*zakāh*), pilgrimage is one of the pillars of Islam. It consists of a journey to Mecca and the performance of a number of highly symbolic rites and rituals around the city.

The *ḥajj* begins at home, where preparations have to be made for the journey. Before the advent of air travel, the journey meant a long period of absence from family and friends. This implied that provisions (*zād*) for the journey had to take account of the long, treacherous journey itself as well as a prolonged absence from home. Islamic legal requirements, therefore, insist that a person who prepares for the pilgrimage must settle debts and leave sufficient resources for dependants. Pilgrimage can be postponed or even cancelled for the sake of one's parents, for example. Preparation for the journey also takes on moral and religious significance. Before the actual departure, a pilgrim visits family and friends and seeks their forgiveness for both known and unintentional acts that may have transpired between them. The pilgrim is getting ready to stand in front of God, and does not want that encounter to be sullied by less than perfect human relations. A perfect pilgrimage leads to complete absolution of sins, and nobody would want to mar such an expectation by neglecting to resolve inter-human friction. A well-known *ḥadīth* of the Prophet underlies this important part of the *ḥajj* preparation:

> On the authority of 'Ā'ishah, the Prophet said: There are three registers: a register of that which is forgiven by God; a register of that which God does not forgive; and register from which nothing is ever omitted . . . as for the register from which nothing is ever omitted, it is the list of wrongs committed by His servants against their fellow human beings.
>
> (Quoted in al-Jīlānī 1995: II, 150)

The only way to improve one's record in the third register is to seek forgiveness from the injured persons themselves. Having made both the material and moral preparation, the journey to Mecca may begin. In earlier times it followed the familiar caravan routes to Mecca, but today other routes have been mapped in contemporary *ḥajj*.

At certain marked stages (*mīqāt*) depending on where one comes from, the pilgrim pauses and places him- or herself in *iḥrām*. The latter is a verbal noun and refers to turning oneself into an inviolable state when entering the inviolable space (*ḥaram*) of Mecca. The pilgrim can be said to be taking on the characteristic of the *ḥaram* during which he or she must observe taboos and avoid certain acts like cutting hair or hunting. The act itself consists of a ritual bath (*ghusl*), a change of clothing, and two cycles of prayer. For men, the clothing of *iḥrām* consists of two pieces of unseamed cloth, one wrapped around the waist and one bound over the left shoulder and leaving the right shoulder bare. Women must not wear a face veil. Many Muslim cultures have also included the wearing of white for women during the *ḥajj* itself. For both men and women, the *iḥrām* represents an important stage in the pilgrimage. At the very least, it breaks the journey at a crucial point and orientates the pilgrims for the next stage.

The *ḥajj* proper consists of five days of ritual obligations. The first day, the eighth of Dhu'l-ḥijja, begins in Mecca with rituals at the Sacred House. In particular, the pilgrim performs a circumambulation (*ṭawāf*) around the Ka'bah located in the centre of the House. One *ṭawāf* consists of seven circular movements around the Ka'bah in an anti-clockwise direction (see Figure 3). The *ṭawāf* is followed by the rite of *sa'y*

Figure 3 Pilgrims performing the circumambulation of the Ka'bah in Mecca

(hastening) between two pillars in the sanctuary. In between the two rites, one drinks water from the well of Zamzam. These rites enact the important biblical narrative, from an Islamic perspective, recalling the occasion when the patriarch Abraham left Hagar and her son, Ishmael, in the desert. In the epic foundation myth of Abraham, the original *muslim*, he was instructed by God to leave his second wife and son at the present site of Mecca. Undeterred by the absence of water, both Abraham and Hagar accepted God's command and expressed their complete faith and belief in their creator. The *ṭawāf* seven times around the Ka'bah symbolizes that same sentiment. The great mystic poet Rūmī wrote the following quatrains to emphasize the deeply symbolic nature of the ritual:

> The wheel of heaven, with all its pomp and splendour,
> circles around God like a mill
> My soul, circumambulate around such a Ka'ba; beggar,
> circle about such a table
> Travel like a ball around in His polo-field, inasmuch as you
> have become happy and helpless.
>
> (Quoted in Arberry 1968: 31)

Once left alone, when her child asked for water Hagar began her quest for sustenance. Her *sa'y* (running) from one hill to another is a symbol of the necessary role of striving and seeking daily sustenance. In spite of an unquestioned devotion to and trust in God, human beings have to seek sustenance. The ritual of *sa'y* symbolizes both the running of Hagar and the daily quest in which we must all engage. Hagar's search and striving was rewarded with miraculous water gushing out from under her son, which today continues to flow from the well of Zamzam. If the *sa'y* represents the effort required to live in this world, then the water of Zamzam represents the grace that accompanies and crowns such a striving. Like Hajar, our sustenance from God will not fail us, but we have both to strive for and to depend on God at the same time.

The pilgrim then proceeds to Mina, and on the next day goes to the plain of Arafat, located a few miles south of Mecca. This rite involves a gathering of all the pilgrims in an open, flat valley. Arafat is the site of a ritual of 'standing' (*wuqūf*) in which pilgrims are free to meditate, worship, and supplicate. They are even encouraged to combine the noon and later afternoon prayers, making more room for private devotion. Standing at Arafat is regarded as the most important part of pilgrimage.

From a juridical perspective, one's presence at Arafat is the most efficacious part of pilgrimage. Taking a step back from these ritual requirements, we note that the journey to God has been continuous and has ended with oneself in the presence of God and a multitude of similarly motivated individuals. I have argued that the journey to a mosque leads one to a pilgrimage to Mecca. On arrival at Mecca, the high point of the pilgrimage now lies outside the city. Like the *miḥrāb* of the mosque, the Sacred House of Mecca was another stage in the journey. It too has to be transcended when one makes the pilgrimage. And at Arafat, there is really nothing – and everything – for which one came, as one stands in the presence of God, one's true presence.

The closest echoes of standing at Arafat in the Islamic tradition are the two extremities of human existence. At the beginning, God called up humankind for the original covenant:

> When your Lord gathered all of Adam's children and had them testify 'Am I not your Lord?' and they answered 'Yes, we accept.' This, so that you cannot say on the day of judgement that we were not aware of this.
>
> (Qur'ān 7: 122)

This meeting of primordial souls at the dawn of their existence took place at a 'moment' pregnant with significance. The Day of Arafat ultimately recalls that moment in life. Similarly, at the primordial end of time, the Day of Judgement also presents itself as a meeting of momentous proportion:

> The day on which the Spirit and the angels stand in rows. None shall speak except one given permission by the Most Merciful, and then speak the truth. That is the true day.
>
> (Qur'ān 78:38–9)

The Day of Arafat brings together in a powerful rite both these highly important events, spanning creation and by implication the life of every individual, from beginning to end. It brings together the existential significance of the primordial covenant as well as the final reckoning of the self with its Maker. The openness and emptiness of Arafat is filled with meaningful space and a meaningful moment between self and God; between self and the greater Self. Such a moment of loneliness and fullness with God has inspired many an Islamic poet and author. Thus, Ibn al-Fāriḍ (d. 1235), the great Cairene poet, said: 'I have been alone with the Beloved and we shared secrets which meant more than the breeze when night comes' (quoted by Smith 1950: 96).

The rite of standing ends at sunset, after which the pilgrims proceed to Mina. On the way, they pause for a while at *al-mash'ar al-ḥarām*, a site at Muzdalifa, east of Mecca, where they pick up forty-nine or seventy pebbles for the next rite. When the next day breaks, they descend into the valley of Mina and throw seven pebbles at the largest of the three stone obelisks called the *al-jamrah al-'aqabah*. These edifices represent the devil, Shayṭān, and recall the story of Abraham, who had set out to sacrifice his son in accordance with the orders of God. As Abraham led his son for the sacrifice, the devil tried to dissuade him from carrying out the act. He argued, quite reasonably, that God would not expect him to carry out such an act. But Abraham stood firm, and the devil approached Hagar and Ismail in succession. Each of them repelled and rejected his advances by the symbolic thowing of pebbles. This narrative very clearly illustrates the key characteristic of the devil as a deceiver, sometimes referred to as Deception itself. He is not necessarily evil personified, standing against the Goodness of God. Rather, the battle between good and evil rages within the human self, the choice lying between the true self that turns towards truth and goodness, and self-deception, represented by Satan. The family of Abraham, the father of prophets, shows human beings how to respond to the Deceiver, and the pilgrims who throw these pebbles resolve to resist the temptations of the Deceiver.

The day is not over without the sacrifice of an animal, again, a symbolic sacrifice of one's desires for the sake of God. The final ritual act is the removal of at least some portion of hair. It is recommended that men remove all the hair from the head; women snip a few strands. The ritual releases one from the state of inviolability (*iḥrām*). Pilgrims then proceed to Mecca to perform another round of *ṭawāf* and the *sa'y*, completing the cyclical and thus continuous journey: Mecca–Mina–Arafat–Mina. However, they return to Mina for the next two or three days, the particular choice lying with the individual pilgrim. On the following days, the remaining pebbles are thrown (seven at a time) at the three stone edifices. The remaining days in Mina are an occasion to continue with the remembrance of God: as the Qur'ān says, as you 'used to remember your forefathers, but even with greater devotion' (Qur'ān 2: 199). This particular reference indicates the extent to which pre-Islamic Arab practices were incorporated into the religious rituals of Islam. The establishment of Islam, of course, was a departure from many of the social and religious practices in Arabia, but it did not complete eliminate the formal structures of the society. The pilgrimage, in particular, was an Islamization of old customs, with new meanings infused into the old.

The stay at Mina is a period of relative relaxation, as there are not too many ritual expectations. Pilgrims have the time to meet people from all over the world. Mina, in this sense, is truly an international gathering of cultures and languages, united by the fact that pilgrims have come to affirm and experience absolution, devotion and surrender to God. *Ḥajj* is regarded as a powerful symbol of the unity of Muslims across racial, linguistic and national boundaries. As people approach Mecca from all corners of the globe, they symbolically reinforce the basic humanity of all peoples. The meeting of different peoples is certainly unmistakable and moving. The level of accommodation and compromise with idiosyncracies, barring a few exceptions, is something that should not be brushed aside. However, the barrier of language and cultures cannot be broken in two or three days, and Mina is more a symbol of Muslim unity than a reality, although if we consider the opportunity for Islamic scholars who share a common language and intellectual disciplines, then its possibilities are greatly enhanced. One can imagine how in the past, when pilgrimage had to include long periods of stay, scholars could share and discuss issues, perhaps even show off their mettle. The early *ḥajj* was an important means by which 'Islamic public opinion' was created, important in the creation of the *ummah* (community) (Pearson 1994: 68). More recently, the *ḥajj* has become the site for contemporary Islamic movements that wish to gather forces. Thus, the revolutionary Iranian ideologue, Ali Shariati (d. 1977) has suggested that pilgrims are provided with the opportunity to meet and engage with each other at Mina:

> Why should more than a million people remain in this valley for two or three more days? This time allows them to think about *ḥajj* and understand what they have done. They can discuss their problems with people from other parts of the world who have the same faith, love, needs and ideology. Muslim thinkers and intellectuals who gather here and freedom-fighters who fight colonialism, oppression, poverty, ignorance and corruption in their homelands, get to know each other.
>
> (Shariati 1980: 109)

It is interesting to note that in spite of this unity, there are no rituals to be performed in congregation during *ḥajj*. There is no Friday sermon or communal meal, for example. The pilgrims perform the same rituals at the same times and places, but their performances are never dependent on each other. In its essential feature, pilgrimage consists of a set of rituals that engage the individual, his or her devotion, striving, and utter relationship with God, and yet, as a congregation of a multitude of languages, races and nations, the individual pilgrims do represent a group.

When the pilgrims return to Mecca, they immediately prepare to depart. Pilgrims perform a farewell *ṭawāf* and set off back to where they have come from. It is considered to be particularly meritorious to hasten back home. With one's obligations fulfilled and one's spiritual resources brimming, one must go back to the battles of daily life. Like the Prophet Muhammad who experienced revelation and returned to the streets of Mecca, so too must the pilgrims return to the world and engage themselves in struggle. Pilgrimage is a highly fulfilling religious experience, but one that must be followed by a renewed devotion to the world and its moral transformation.

This need to return home does not mean that one cannot first pay a visit to the Prophet. Many pilgrims sometimes proceed to Medina, the city of the Prophet, for a number of days. This visit is not part of the pilgrimage proper, but Medina is regarded as the second most important city in Islam. To go on pilgrimage and neglect a visit to Medina would be regarded as discourteous. From the perspective of Islam as a historically located religion, of course, a visit to Medina is more than just a courteous social obligation. The devotion to the Prophet for legal and religious inspiration and direction is now translated into a ritual visit in its own right. Pilgrims 'greet' the tomb of the Prophet and go to the various historical places in Medina. They visit the first mosque established in Islam, in Qubā; the battlefields around Medina where the early Muslim community had to defend itself against the mighty Quraysh; and the mosque where the *qiblah* was changed from Jerusalem to Mecca. Some also get a chance to visit the well of 'Uthmān and the garden of Salmān, two key Companions in the life of the Prophet.

Most Muslims read about the city of the Prophet in biographies and songs of praise. For example, the devotional singers of Pakistan (*qawwāl*) continually remind devotees that they are on their way to Medina (*Madineh chalo* in Urdu). More generally, a genre of biographical writing about the Prophet started soon after his death and has continued unabated into the twentieth century. Through these many cultural forms, almost every aspect of the life of the Prophet, and by extension, his city, is deeply ingrained in the life of a Muslim. Newby's summation of the earliest biography captures the seminal role of the Prophetic biography in Islamic life:

> In the Sīrah [Prophetic biographical work], Ibn Isḥāq helped form an image of Muḥammad that accounted for the rise of Islam, explained the course of the history of the world, established the primacy of the Qur'ānic text as scripture, and installed Muḥammad as the central religious authority for Muslims.
>
> (Newby 1989: 2)

Since then, Muslims have continued to expresses their unique position in world religious history in relation to the Prophet and his city. The proper etiquette for approaching the city was prescribed for those fortunate to make it there, while others longed for a glimpse of the radiant city (*al-madīnah al-munawwarah*). Jāmī, the great Persian poet (d. 1492), exhibits the special place of Medina in the hearts of all Muslims:

> It is we who, like the tulip in the desert of Medina,
> Bear in our heart the scar of longing for Medina.
> Passionate longing for Paradise may disappear from the
> wise man's head, but
> It is not possible that the passionate longing for Medina
> should leave him.
>
> (Quoted in Schimmel 1985: 191)

In short, if Mecca is a centre of the House of God where one confronts one's relationship with God and self, then the itinerary in Medina defines the historical foundation of the first Muslim community. The visit to the green-domed tomb of Muhammad and all the other significant places in the city is a profound initiation into the Islamic sense of place that Muslims experience as a community, and which the pilgrims experience as they trace their steps around the city's significant spots. As they pray in the Prophet's mosque and walk in his city, they feel reaffirmed in the historical community of believers of which they are an integral part.

THE MUSLIM COMMUNITY

I have argued that the pilgrimage powerfully reaffirms the meaning of the international Islamic community and that the *ummah* is also firmly located in the pilgrims' visit to the city of the Prophet. Both practices emphasize and reinforce, ritually and in their accompanying narratives, the global and transcending nature of the *ummah*. This particular meaning of the *ḥajj* leads us to consider the nature of this international *ummah*, its possibilities and its limitations. We begin with the meaning and historical foundation of the concept, and then proceed to its modern predicament.

The word *ummah* has several meanings in the Qur'ān. In some places, it refers to the whole of humanity as a single group: 'Humankind was a single *ummah*' (2: 213). One source of subsequent division within the single unit of humankind was the varying responses towards prophets and messengers sent by God. In the following verse, the Qur'ān also refers to a single human individual as an *ummah*: 'Verily, Abraham was a committed *ummah* to you' (Qur'ān 2:128). And in a third usage of the term, *ummah* refers to a moral code: 'We found our forefathers with an *ummah* and followed them' (Qur'ān 43:22). *Ummah*, then, may be a reference to a distinct moral quality which can be applied to an individual, a group, or to humankind as a whole. The term stresses the ethical consciousness at the root of humankind. Not only the individual, but the community too, takes on a moral character in its responsibility towards God.

The *ummah* as a historical community with a certain set of beliefs was crystallized in the life of the Prophet, particularly when he arrived in Medina. The first mosque was established and rituals and laws were laid down for the new community. This community was, in the context of Arabia, a supra-tribal community which took its identity and nature from its connection to the Prophet of God. As soon as the Prophet arrived in Medina, he concluded an agreement among the various tribes which accentuated the social and political implications of this new *ummah*. In a *ṣaḥīfah* (treatise) of Medina, the Prophet Muhammad drew up an agreement between the various groups of Muslims: 'this is a letter (*kitāb*) from Muhammad between the believers of the Quraysh and the people of Yathrib and whoever follows them and fights with them, that they are one community (*ummah*) to the exclusion of everybody else' (Hamidullah 1969: 41). In this agreement, each tribe accepted Muhammad as the final arbiter of disputes, and committed itself to engage with the others on the basis of justice and moral aptness (*qisṭ* and *ma'ruf*), particularly in relation to blood feuds and disputes. In spite of the unity of purpose proposed in the document, however, individual tribes were not eliminated or denied their identities. While their religious commitment was regarded as a higher symbol of belonging, they maintained their identities. It is this form of universal community that is manifested in the *ḥajj* as it reflects both the unity and diversity of the Islamic *ummah*.

Two aspects of this universal community must be emphasized, because they are often overlooked in modern discussions of Islam. The first relates to the fact that the treatise strikes a balance between the unity and cohesiveness of the group under the leadership of Muhammad on the one hand, and the continuing validity of tribal identities on the other. The overarching unity is built both around the leadership of the Prophet and the values of justice and moral aptness. Group identities are thus not simply transcended but prioritized by political arrangement (leadership) and ethical values. The *ummah* takes shape in the context of higher values, but the continuing validity of the smaller groups is as powerful as the unifying force overarching them. This aspect of the *ummah* seems to elude many contemporary scholars of Islam who see no fundamental basis for the value of local identities in an Islamic *ummah*.

For example, the al Fārūqīs are correct in pointing out the new *ummah* as a cross-cultural and inter-religious body when they say that the 'Pax Islamica' was

> laid down in a permanent constitution by the Prophet in Madīnah in the first days of the *hijrah* (emigration). He made it inclusive of the Jews of Madīnah and Christians of Najran, guaranteeing to them their identity and their religious, social and cultural institutions.
>
> (al Fārūqī and al Fārūqī 1986: 84–5)

For the al Fārūqīs, however, Muslim *ummah* has transcended the inter-tribal boundaries completely and comprehensively:

> believers are a single brotherhood, whose members mutually love one another in God, who cause one another to do justice and be patient . . . [who share] a tripartite consensus of mind, heart and arm. There is consensus in their thought, in their decision, in their attitude and character, and in their arms. It is a universal brotherhood which knows neither colour nor ethnic identity. In its purview, all men are one, measurable only in terms of piety.
>
> (1986: 84–5)

This conceptualization of Islam is shared by critical outside observers like Bernard Lewis, an authority on political developments in modern Islam. Lewis denies any place to non-religious identities within the Muslim *ummah*: 'descent, language, and habitation were all of secondary importance, and it is only during the last century that, under European influence, the concept of the political nation has begun to make headway' (Lewis: 1966: 71). According to Lewis, only the religious aspect of Islam, not ethnicity or political ideologies, appeals to the mass of Muslims in the modern world: 'the religious orders alone spring from the native soil, and express the passions of the submerged masses of the population' (ibid.). The values of 'secondary importance', which Lewis acknowledges, are completely lost in this observation.

Both the al Fārūqīs and Lewis suppress or ignore the dynamics of the first treatise in Medina, in which tribal groups were affirmed. Moreover, subsequent Islamic history cannot be read without regard to the dynamics between Islam as a transcending belief-system and the cultures and languages that make up the *ummah* mosaic. In fact, when one goes beyond the political rhetoric of Muslim activists and those observers who see Muslims as one seamless body of religious devotees, the vitality of local cultures that permeate the Muslim *ummah* cannot be missed. This is evident in the *ḥajj*, the supreme ritual and symbol of the universal community of believers. When Muslims come together for pilgrimage, they are certainly manifesting the 'ummatic' aspect of Islam. However, regional identities are not denied but rather crystallized in the process. Thus the contemporary Moroccan identity, it has been argued by El Moudden, took shape when greater numbers of Moroccans made the pilgrimage. Within Morocco itself, the difference between class and ethnicity, between high and low, would be clearly felt. On pilgrimage, however, these differences became submerged as a Moroccan identity emerged and was expressed in *ḥajj* travel accounts. Pilgrimage, it seems, was, paradoxically, also contributing to local identities (El Moudden 1990). This 'national' character was also noticed by a South African pilgrim during a fire that swept through the makeshift tents of Mina during the *ḥajj* of 1997. As families were broken up in the evacuation, the South African pilgrims were attracted to a quick-thinking pilgrim who raised the new South African flag.

The pilgrimage, in spite of its profound symbols, does not completely deny local identities. People from the same geographical area or language group, for example, meet and identify with each other. In Mina and other places in the pilgrimage, people from a particular country coalesce together, but they remain noticeable, as in the following account of a 1922 pilgrimage:

> Color and race and rank, like the distance of land and sea, yield to the supreme purpose, make the world of the pilgrim move in a common faith toward a goal unique [but] From every ship a scene, from every land a fashion. The Takruri black, a giant with a rag around his loins; the fastidious Somali in florid gingham apron and white toga; the Javanese with their unveiled women in short skirts of gorgeous colours or just a piece of rich material clinging to their stunted forms; the gentlemen from India, in graceful folds of silk and cashmere, traveling third class with the multitude; the fellah of Egypt in red slippers and blue gallabiyyah; the trans-Caucasian in a huge turban crowning a truculency of aspect unassuaged; and the Moroccan, graceful and stately and proud, in the ample folds of an immaculate white bornous . . .
>
> (Quoted in Peters 1994: 339–40)

In spite of this pilgrim's obvious bad taste and manner, it is truly remarkable to see how such diversity is manifested and held together in the pilgrimage. This diversity is denied because it is so often overlooked in the quest for pure ideologies.

Beyond the pilgrimage, local identities may also be noticeable in the development of Islamic cultures. While Arabic is regarded, like the *ḥajj*, as a lingua franca that holds the *ummah* together, the history of Islam has also produced cultures and languages richly imbued with the values of Islam. It is unthinkable to speak of the richness of Islamic thought without taking into consideration Persian poetry, for example. Modern Sufi movements would not be complete without the Mouridiyyah in Senegal and its Wolof griots. The Swahili culture of the East African coast, the Urdu *ghazals* and *qawwālī* (devotional songs) of India, and the unique blend of Islam and Hindu arts in Indonesia, are all part of the *ummah* mosaic. The centre is always present, certainly, to influence and bind the cultures together, but the peripheries acquire their uniqueness in the process.

The second aspect of the *ummah* that calls for our attention is the preoccupation with the religious dimension of the *ummah*, overlooked by many moderns, Muslim and non-Muslim alike. In Islamic history, of course, the *ummah* has become the community of believers, which excludes those who do not believe. It is instructive to remember, though, that these boundaries were not always as clear as they are made out to be. The *ummatic* character of humankind is present in the Qur'ān. As I have argued, this refers to the inherent moral nature of human individuals and communities. In this regard, the human *ummah* consists of groups who respond differently to the moral call of the Prophet. This notion of *ummah* as a overarching community of human beings, and not simply believers of a particular religion, is evident in the *ṣaḥifah* of the first community of believers established by the Prophet. The agreement also included among the people of Medina those who had not yet become Muslims (Hamidullah 1968: 21). This agreement established the Prophet as a leader in the community, and individual tribal members, who were not yet Muslims, were represented by their groups. They were not excluded on the basis of their being non-Muslims. The matter becomes more fascinating when we look at a similar agreement between the Prophet and the Jews of Medina. The latter are declared to be an 'an *ummah* with the believers', which is also extremely suggestive (Hamidullah 1968: 44). Some scholars have argued that there is a huge difference between being 'with the *ummah*' and being the *ummah* itself. I do not want to deny the deeply religious nature of this community formation, but it seems as if the *ummah* was an expression of a political agreement at one time, and of a religious and political agreement at other times. The first agreement between the Prophet and the Arabs of Medina defined the *ummah* as both a religious and political community, and included tribal members who had not yet joined the new religion. On the other hand, the *ummah* of the Muslims and the Jews was a political arrangement, without completely excluding the religious and moral dimension of *ummah*. If we appeal to the Qur'ānic notion of human responsibility, then there were two simultaneous notions of *ummah*: one consisting of Muslims and the other of a political community of sorts. The underlying basis of *ummah*, then, is the moral sense of humanity. In Islamic history, and contemporary discussion of Islam, the concept has become the preserve of Muslims only.

The *miḥrāb* in the mosque led into the fascinating issue of how Muslims reach God. The different religious tendencies, theological, mystical and philosophical, were regarded as various attempts to respond to God and his prophets. In ritual form, the search for God is best represented in Islam by the pilgrimage. It represents a journey and a search for God which becomes a basis for a shared commitment and community. The pilgrimage, however, is also a powerful symbol of the community (*ummah*) that straddles cultural and national boundaries. This has led us into considering the unity and diversity within Islam as communal expression.

5 THE *MINBAR*
Power and authority in Islam

Is it not sufficient that you are standing while the people are sitting?
(Ibn Khaldūn n. d.: 297)

This striking comment from the second caliph of Islam, ʻUmar, was sent to his governor in Egypt who wanted to build a raised platform from which to address the congregation in the mosque. It is an intriguing but powerful statement about leadership in Islam. The ambiguity and precariousness of Islamic leadership implied in the remark is not often acknowledged or recognized. The power of religious leaders, particularly in modern Islam, comes close to resembling natural hierarchies in a religious structure. We shall use its physical location in the mosque in order to explore the meaning of leadership in Islam. Following the symbols inside the mosque, we shall examine the principal models and ideal types of leadership in Islam, and close with how leadership remains as precarious as it was in ʻUmar's rhetorical warning to his governor.

MINBAR AND *MIḤRĀB*

Authority and leadership are inextricably part of the religion, a part for which the *minbar* (pulpit) in the mosque is the most powerful symbol. The Prophet established Friday worship as soon as he reached Medina, even before he built the central mosque. The Friday service is distinguished from other daily prayers by the presence of a sermon (*khuṭbah*), which literally means 'an address'. The purpose of the *minbar* is to provide a structure from which to address the congregation in a sermon, most commonly on Fridays but also on other occasions.

Addressing the congregation from a central place in the mosque was an important function of the Prophetic office. This was the symbol of the Prophet's leadership and authority. It was the focal point for a weekly pattern, as much as the five prayers organized the day. In fact, it is possible that the name of the sacred scripture in Islam is a *qur'ān*, literally a recitation, because it was announced and recited on such a public platform. I am not suggesting that the text cannot be read for individual study or devotion, nor that all the verses were first publicly recited on a Friday, but the Friday sermon is the most important place for the recitation of the Qur'ān. In a study of a modern preacher in Jordan, Antoun captures its pervasive presence: 'But the most regular and significant recitation of the Qur'ān is on the occasion of the Friday congregational prayer service. Recitation precedes the Friday sermon and follows it, and the preacher punctuates his sermons with appropriate verses as does the worshipper in the culminating Friday congregational prayer' (Antoun 1989: 6). The recitation of the Qur'ān occupies a central role in the sermon and, in turn, denotes that the location from which the word of God is recited to the world is an important and authoritative place in the mosque. It is no wonder the *minbar* and the sermon exude authority as no other symbols in Islam.

When the Prophet died, the office of leader was taken over by the caliphs and then, in their name, by scholars. It was not a smooth transition, and the story will be explored to some extent in this chapter. However, this seemingly unequivocal role and place of the leader in Islam must be contrasted with his uneasy ritual location. The *minbar*'s leadership connotation is matched by the deep sense of egalitarianism in the mosque. This point can be illustrated very clearly in the contrast between worship and preaching in their respective physical locations in the mosque. When the *imām* leads the congregation in worship, he stands on the same level as his followers, facing as they do in the direction of Mecca. When he addresses the congregation in a sermon, however, he stands on a raised platform with his back against the wall, facing the people. From a functional point of view, the raised platform is simply a means for carrying the voice of the speaker beyond the initial rows of the congregation. From a symbolic point of view, the physiology of the two places in the mosque implies radically different leadership roles. In this regard, the opening quotation from 'Umar indicates a concern that the *minbar* symbol, exploiting the powerful notion of height, may endanger the symbol of the leader standing with the congregation. The *minbar* in Islam potentially threatens the *miḥrāb*, and vice versa.

It may surprise many Muslims to know that in fact there was disagreement among early scholars as to the requirement for a sermon at Friday worship. Most regarded it as an essential part of the Friday prayer, but others, like the great theologian and highly respected ascetic Ḥasan al-Baṣrī (d. 728), regarded it as a recommended aspect of the Friday service only (Sābiq 1980: I, 230). This may have been a direct response to the Umayyad practice of setting the sermon apart from the public. The Umayyads have the dubious distinction of having introduced beautiful *maqṣūrah*s into mosques, from within which the sermon could be delivered (see Figure 4). These structures were ornately designed thrones which were completely closed and inaccessible to the regular worshippers. The preacher, the symbol of leadership, would enter the *maqṣūrah* and ascend its flight of stairs. Once he was inside, the *maqṣūrah* door would be closed and guarded by soldiers. Hence the *maqṣūrah* may be regarded as the logical outcome of the standing above the heads of the believers about which 'Umar warned his governor. The *maqṣūrah*, beautiful as it may appear, is in complete contrast to a leader standing in front of his congregation with his back to them.

The statement of 'Umar and the juristic debate about the importance of the sermon reflect competing views of leadership. In this regard, it seems that while worship was a non-negotiable aspect of the community, the sermon as a powerful symbol of leadership was contested. The ambiguity of height, first noted in this work in the discussion of the minaret in Islam, never disappeared. The juxtaposition of leadership and believers, height and ground level, occurs again and again in Islam. When we turn from the local mosque to the Meccan sanctuary, the height of the Ka'bah raised above ground level also became a point of contention. The issue was raised when the authority of the early Umayyad dynasty was challenged by the Prophet's early Companions, opening up the question of leadership in Islam. The next section will unpack this complex but important dimension of Islam.

MODELS OF LEADERSHIP

After his demise, the Prophet's successors followed him in both his religious and socio-political leadership. They continued his religious

Figure 4 Maqṣūrah *in the Furuq Mosque, Khartoum*

office, not in the sense of continuing prophecy, but in their role as prayer leaders, preachers, and models of piety and righteousness. Most Muslims believe that such a state of affairs continued until the Umayyads came to power under the leadership of Mu'āwiyah and his successors. When this happened, it unleashed a series of questions about leadership and society which continue to be felt in contemporary Muslim societies. The history of early Islam is much more complex than the outline I shall be presenting here, but it will suffice for our purpose of delineating the key models of leadership in Islam. My approach will be to explore these models as they emerged in the course of certain historical events. My primary reason for recounting the history is not the events themselves, but the exemplars of leadership that were shaped in them.

Our search begins with the dispute that arose at the close of the 'righteous caliphate' about thirty years after the death of the Prophet. The meaning and nature of this formative period was very much defined by what happened later in Islamic history, as ideals were conceptualized in relation to the terrible reality. As history is told and retold, it becomes overlaid with perceptions and ideologies which are impossible to dislocate from 'what really happened'. Nevertheless, it is still possible to delineate some key features of this early history in order to highlight the leadership symbols and values that inspire and motivate Muslims. The righteous caliphate (*al-khilāfah al-rāshidah*) denotes the first four caliphs who succeeded the Prophet Muhammad. This period has been portrayed in Muslim historical consciousness, particularly by the majority Sunnis, as a period exemplifying right conduct and moral rectitude. The righteous caliphs were, in order of succession, Abū Bakr, 'Umar, 'Uthmān and 'Alī. Some Shi'ites accept only the first two caliphs, Abū Bakr and 'Umar, while most Shi'ites restrict the ideal period to the reign of 'Alī only.

Unfortunately, this golden period did not last long, and began to falter when the Umayyads began to ease their way into the body politic of Islam. Some of this, in fact, happened during the period of the righteous caliphate. Mu'āwiyah was first appointed as a governor of Greater Syria by 'Umar, the second caliph. However, he rose to prominence when he refused to accept the leadership of 'Alī, the fourth caliph or first Shi'ite Imām. In some respects, his accession to a leading position in society meant that the leadership of the Muslim community was passing on to the erstwhile foes of the Prophet. Mu'āwiyah's father, Abū Sufyān, was one of the bitterest foes of Islam until the conquest of

Mecca. The reclamation of leadership in the religious order they opposed for so long did not bode well. At the very least, their rise put the people of Medina, the loyal followers of the Prophet, into a quandary. These leaders were clearly Muslims but they were also reasserting the authority of the old Arab aristocracy.

Mu'āwiyah was able to hold on to power, and perhaps, as a religious scholar, even generate some legitimacy for his rule. At the end of his career, however, he appointed his son Yazīd as his successor and laid the foundation of dynastic rule in Islamic politics. Yazīd's appointment immediately led to revolt as he was known to be iniquitous in his personal behaviour as well as in his commitment to the tenets of the faith. To many, this was a classic case of a revolution suffering a severe reversal. The earliest Companions of the Prophet were also incensed, but they differed as to how to deal with the situation. Some advocated carrying arms against Yazīd while others preferred withdrawal from all political and social disputes in the *ummah*. These responses established the particular religious groups among Muslims that continue today. In the context of our discussion here, they established leadership models within Islamic society.

LEADERSHIP OF POWER

Let us begin with the conception of the rulers themselves, the Umayyads, who, whether they were accepted or not, maintained their roles as both the political and religious leaders of the community. They expected absolute obedience and deference as both the successors of the Prophet and as the vicegerents of God on earth. In fact, they seem to have regarded themselves as more vicegerents of God than successors to the Prophet. In a letter of designation of his successor, one of the later Umayyad cailiphs, Walīd II (743–4), argued that the Prophet 'deputed his caliphs over the path of his prophethood (*'alā minhāj nubuwwatihi*) for the implementation of his decree, the establishment of his normative practice (*sunnah*)' and insisted that 'obedience is the head of this matter, its summit, its apex, its halter, its foundations, its refuge and its mainstay' (quoted in Crone 1986: 120, 121). One of the well-known generals of the Umayyads, Ḥajjāj b. Yūsuf, even went as far as to say that 'the caliphs of God on earth are nobler that the messenger sent to them' (Crone 1986: 28). While the early caliphs regarded themselves as successors to Muhammad, the Umayyads were more ambitious. They exploited the symbolism in the word 'caliph' (*khalīfah*: a deputy) over against the term 'messenger' (*rasūl*). In the ordinary sense of the terms, the deputies of God, they argued, were better than the messengers of God. In royal terms, the deputies enjoyed a greater eminence than messengers.

More than the royal meaning of deputy, the Umayyad sense of leadership drew on the significance of the *khalīfah* in Islamic text. The word may simply denote a successor in the sense of a person who comes after (*khalf*) another. In this sense, Abū Bakr was a successor (*khalīfah*) of the Prophet in that he took control of the reins of government after him. However, it may also denote a sense of special eminence enjoyed potentially by all humans, and actually by prophets. This second, more exalted notion of *khalīfah* comes from the following verse in the Qur'ān: 'And when your Lord said to the angels that I am going to place a *khalīfah* on earth' (Qur'ān 2:30). The next verses go on to outline the special eminence of humanity as potentially superior creatures, even though they may occasionally display a propensity to 'sow destruction on the earth and spill blood'. Reflecting on this notion of humanity, Nasr stated:

> Islam without in any way overlooking the limited and weak aspect of human nature does not consider man in his aspect as a perverted will but essentially as a theomorphic being who as the vicegerent (*khalīfah*) of God on earth is the central theophany (*tajalli*) of God's names and qualities.
> (Nasr 1994: 18)

The Umayyad concept of authority conflated this exalted potential of all humanity into the persons who actually ruled over the Islamic territories. They used this notion of 'caliph' to transcend the messenger. They themselves were not quite prophets, but their authority emulated, competed with and went beyond that of the Prophet. Apart from the theological problem inherent in this formulation, such a position seems to combine the symbolic power of the *khalīfah* in the Qur'ān and the actual power held by leaders. Without any discussion of values and criteria for judging authority, this conflation seems a long way from the religious and political authority exemplified by the Prophet Muhammad. It indicates how political and religious authority within the personality of one ruler could become its own justification. By virtue of being a caliph, a leader was inherently suited to rule and commanded absolute obedience like the Prophet himself.

This is a far cry from the position taken by 'Umar in his letter to his governor, but it is one that has prevailed in Islam. It was a position initiated by the Umayyads, but it has since been replicated by successive Muslim dynasties, rulers and contemporary monarchies. In the dynasties established by Muslim rulers, the balance between authority and egalitarianism was completely lost. Political authority and dominance was a recognized form of leadership, accepted and justified in religious terms. Al-Jāḥiẓ (d. 868), writing in support of the Abbasid caliphs who followed the Umayyads, said that it was absolutely necessary to have one legitimate political ruler, someone who was intelligent, erudite, decisive and possessed good habits (Pellat 1969: 65). Moreover, the ruler should be like the Prophet: 'Respect for God's Messenger requires that only men like him as possible should in each age occupy the position he held ' (Pellat 1969: 65). For al-Jāḥiẓ, this meant that the ruler was a successor to the Prophet, and should adopt his wise and ethical qualities. Not suprisingly, al-Jāḥiẓ locates these qualities in the Hashemites, the family of the Prophet as well as that of the Abbasids (Pellat 1969: 58–64).

This position was not only justified by individuals like al-Jāḥiẓ who sought to support their mentors. It was was also confirmed by other scholars who tried to define the minimum standards required of rulers. Enayat has argued that the political philosophy of many scholars after the end of the righteous caliphate became progressively realist:

> compared with their Shi'i counterparts, the Sunni exponents of the theory of the caliphate between the fifth/eleventh and eighth/fourteenth centuries – not to mention the present period – displayed much greater flexibility in adapting their ideas to political realities. This flexibility eventually reached a point at which the supreme value in politics appeared to be, not justice but security – a state of mind which set a high premium on the ability to rule and maintain 'law and order,' rather than on piety.
>
> (Enayat 1982: 12)

Jurists outlined the minimal requirements expected of a ruler before he could be overthrown. Thus, many maintained that, as long as a person performed daily worship, he ought not to be overthrown for any other kind of wrongdoing. The great Andalusian scholar of Qur'ānic exegesis al-Qurtubī disagreed with this position, but the following statement reveals his suspicion of political claims:

> When a Kharijite rises to fight iniquity it is not for the people to rush to assist [him] until his intention is clarified. [The people should know] that his is a just [cause] and that it is in conformity with the [wishes of the] community to remove the previous [ruler]. This is because he who seek this matter appears to be righteous until he attains power and then returns to his habit contrary to what he had earlier promised.
>
> (al-Qurtubī 1967: I, 271, 273)

One can appreciate the perceptiveness of the scholar with regard to the reality of political leadership and power. The fact of the matter, however, is that this extreme caution led to extreme realism and then to the Islamic justification of power. Thus, Ibn Khaldūn could say in his monumental vision of society and history that 'the sword and the pen are both instruments for the ruler' (Ibn Khaldūn n. d.: 283–4). By this he meant that both scholarship, representing truth and values, and the sword, representing power, were an intrinsic part of Islamic leadership. Leadership, in this configuration, comes with power and may be defined by it.

LEADERSHIP OF PERSONALITY

Fortunately, Islamic leadership is not simply about power. Power is important and cannot be ignored in the evaluation of a society's ethics and values, but it cannot be the only consideration of leadership. Among those who chose to rebel against the Umayyads was 'Abd Allāh b. al-Zubayr, the son of a prominent Companion of the Prophet. He decided to move to the Meccan sanctuary and protest against the accession of the Umayyads. His withdrawal to Mecca was a declaration of a dispute which needed to be resolved. Mecca was universally regarded as a sanctuary (*ḥaram*) where disputes could be resolved without going to war. On the other hand, Ibn al-Zubayr was also concerned about extending his influence among a larger group of Muslims, and soon began to organize a polity in opposition to the Umayyads. He was able to consolidate his position and even gain supporters from other regions. From his position in Mecca, he also brought about a number of changes there, symbolizing his rejection of the hierarchical model of Umayyad rule. The following example of his vision of changing the architecture of the mosque is illustrative of his approach, as well as of the ambiguity of leadership with which I opened the chapter:

> Ibn al-Zubayr said: I bear witness that I have heard 'Ā'ishah say: the Prophet said: 'Your people [the Quraysh] diminished the House when they built it because they could not afford the expense. So they reduced it by some cubits in the direction toward the Hijr, and but for the fact that till recently they were unbelievers, I would myself demolish the Ka'ba and restore the reduced dimensions. I would also make two doors for it (opening) down on ground level, one toward the east for people to enter and one to the west for people to exit. And do you know why your people raised the door?' And 'Ā'ishah said she did not. Muhammad said: 'To make sure that no one but whom they wished would enter it. If they disliked a certain person entering it, they would allow him to climb up and then, when he was about to enter, they would push him and he would fall to the ground . . .' (Quoted from Peters 1994: 62)

Historians say that Ibn al-Zubayr rebuilt the Ka'bah as envisaged by the Prophet. This rebuilding certainly recalls the statement of 'Umar and directly opposes the Umayyad conception of leadership based on hierarchy. The Umayyads, however, would not tolerate Ibn al-Zubayr's eminence in Arabia, and began a series of campaigns against him and his supporters. They finally launched deadly assaults against the Hijaz, pillaging Medina in the process and bombarding Mecca until Ibn al-Zubayr surrendered in 692, having held his ground in Mecca for ten years. His venture has often been overlooked in popular accounts of Islamic history, but it was a formidable attempt to rebuild a community around the Meccan sanctuary and the leadership of the old loyal supporters of the Prophet. The Umayyads rebuilt the Ka'bah as it had been before Ibn al-Zubayr changed it. We may never know exactly what the shape of the Ka'bah ought to be like, but the textual record we have clearly points to the powerful symbolic battles of height and ground level in early Islam. While the Umayyads built their castles and towering monuments and demanded absolute obedience, other Muslims tried to present alternative configurations of leadership.

If Ibn al-Zubayr's leadership model has been overlooked in history, another opponent of Umayyad rule has never been forgotten. Ḥusayn, the grandson of the Prophet, also rejected Umayyad leadership. In comparison with Ibn al-Zubayr, however, Ḥusayn's opposition neither occupied a region nor generated a loyal group of supporters. In terms of emotional sentiment and religious fervour, his bold challenge to iniquity has more than made up for his small group of loyal supporters. Imām Ḥusayn, as he is known through the Islamic world, left the Hijaz and sought his father's supporters in Kufa, Iraq. On his way, he was met by the army of Yazīd at Karbala and killed in a tragic massacre. No one was spared, not even members of his family who had accompanied him. This tragedy has been remembered in Islamic history as an epic battle between good and evil. It is almost universally commemorated and remembered in Muslim societies, but particularly among the Shi'ites. The commemoration has most often been an occasion to mourn the death of the grandson of the Prophet but often too it has inspired revolts and revolutions against injustice and oppression. The most significant recent examples of the latter have been the Islamic Revolution of Iran and the Southern Lebanese revolt against Israeli occupation.

The tragedy of Karbala focused on all that went wrong in early Islam. From the perspective of leadership in Islam, however, it was subsequently argued that the problem did not only arise with the Umayyads in 661. The root of the conflict went back to the very death of the Prophet Muhammad. Then, as later, the right of 'Alī as the designated successor to the Prophet was usurped. Leadership of the Muslims, according to this view, belonged rightfully to the Prophet's family. Opposed both to the Umayyads who established a family dynasty, and also to Ibn al-Zubayr, who represented the leadership of the old loyal supporters of the Prophet, the Shi'ites (literally, partisans) insisted on the leadership of the family of the Prophet, with the rightful inheritance of Prophetic leadership passing though his house, beginning with 'Alī and followed by his two sons and their descendants in a designated line of succession. Leadership therefore belonged to the line of 'Alī and the Prophet's daughter Fāṭimah. From the Shi'ite perspective, true leadership of the family of the Prophet was known and always waiting to take effect. As time went on, this political movement split into various factions and groups. The Twelvers believe in twelve successive Imāms who followed the Prophet, while the Ismā'īlī line of Imāms continues to the present day. All of them, though, regard the family of the Prophet, represented by direct descendents of the Prophets, the designated Imāms, as the true leaders for the Muslim community. Embodying the virtues of Islam, they provide a clear and unambiguous focus for this group.

The leadership of the Imāms, however, went beyond the right person and the right family. When considering the particular leadership model as an analytical category, the focus of Shi'ite leadership revolved around individuals and their exemplary conduct. Against Umayyad power, the piety of the early Imāms became a striking model of leadership for Muslims. This was clear in the devotional preoccupation of some of the early Imāms as well as in the approach adopted in the scholarly elaboration of Islam. According to Shi'ite exegesis, for example, the Imāms enjoyed direct access to the inner meaning of the Qur'ān. They literally embodied the Qur'ān and in the words of Mahmoud Ayoub, 'they are the "speaking" (*nāṭiq*) Qur'ān, while the Qur'ān after the death of the Muhammad remains the "silent" (*ṣāmit*) Qur'ān' (Ayoub 1988: 183). This concept is closely related to a well-known statement made by 'Ā'ishah when she was once asked about the Prophet. She replied: 'His character was the Qur'ān.' Both the wife of the Prophet and Shi'ite exegesis focused on the personal qualities that manifested Qur'ānic characteristics. Both, in fact, show how the person carries the message, and thus the mantle of leadership. This stands in sharp contrast to the power of the Umayyads and, as we shall presently see, the power of knowledge.

This leadership model has meant that some esteem and deference is shown to the descendants of the Prophet simply as a consequence of their blood relationship. The descendants of the Prophet are prominent, and his family is mentioned in every daily worship: 'God, bless Muhammad and the family of Muhammad'. Moreover, children are often given their names as a token of respect and blessing. Many Muslim male twins are called Ḥasan and Ḥusayn, in remembrance of the two grandchildren of the Prophet. This deference to the family of the Prophet goes beyond Shi'ism, as most Muslims recognize the special status of the Prophet. Taking the family of the Prophet as a model, some Islamic societies also recognize and respect the descendents of his close Companions. Thus, some societies boast families of Ṣiddīqīs (from Abū Bakr al-Ṣiddīq, the first caliph), the Farūqīs (from 'Umar al-Farūq, the second caliph) and the like. Each of these have at one time or another enjoyed the prestige and respect that comes with being part of a 'nobility'. Gilsenan, writing about his experiences of Islamic society in the 1960s, spoke of the deference showed towards descendants of the family of the Prophet in Yemen. People in the streets kissed their hands and addressed them by the honorific titles. The rulers of the kingdoms of Jordan and Morocco claim descent from the Prophet, and so did Ayatollah Khomeini. As Gilsenan noted, however, such a special status has been questioned by revolutionary egalitarian philosophies in contemporary Islam. In the 1960s, it was the Arab socialism of Nasser which rejected the special privileges associated with traditional aristocracies. Since then, other groups of Muslims have felt uneasy about conferring special status on contemporary representatives of the Prophet. They still regard the immediate family of the Prophet with special distinction, but are unwilling to adopt the Orwellian dictum that 'all of us are equal, but some are more equal than others' in the twentieth century.

This wider significance of the Shi'ite model of leadership goes even beyond the family of the Prophet. If we focus on the fact that Shi'ism locates leadership in personality, then we can easily identify its affinity with leadership in Sufism as well. A Sufi mentor or *shaykh* becomes a living model of piety and inwardness as he leads a novice to the deeper significance of the self, God and religious symbols. He or she must be connected to the Prophet through a chain of instructors in which each person is an exemplification of piety and righteousness. Only a person who has him- or herself experienced the inner meaning and beauty of the principal teachings of Islam may instruct and train others to achieve similar objectives. Thus, Abū Sa'īd b. Abī al-Khayr (d. 1048) argued convincingly:

> If men wish to draw near to God, they must seek Him in the hearts of men. They should speak well of all men, whether present or absent, and if they themselves seek to be a light to guide others, then, like the sun, they must show the same face to all. To bring joy to a single heart is better than to build many shrines for worship, and to enslave one soul by kindness is worth more than the setting free of a thousand slaves.
>
> (Quoted in Smith 1950: 49)

This profound statement makes it quite clear that leadership consists of the true exemplification of moral and spiritual qualities in a person. Obviously, it is difficult to claim that one can begin training others and assume that one has reached a certain stage of such exemplification. Usually, this will only come about when one's own teacher grants permission. Sometimes, even this is not sufficient. Thus, the great Sufi Junayd (d. 910) would not train others while his own teacher Sārī al-Saqatī (d. 867) was still alive, and then, out of deference to his master, he did not teach and train others until the Prophet himself appeared to him in a dream and instructed him to do so (Abdel-Kader 1962: 8). Nasr composed the general rule: 'In the hands of a master, he (initiate) must be like a corpse in the hands of the worker of the dead without any movement of his own. The master is the representative of the Prophet and through him of God' (Nasr 1991: 63). And to conclude with Rūmī on this issue: 'Without the power imperial of Shams ul-Haqq of Tabriz, one could neither behold the moon nor become the sea' (quoted in Nasr 1991: 58).

When a person has acquired the degree of the light of which the Shi'ites or Sufis speak then he may be said to exude the *barakah* of God. This concept in Islam may be translated as grace, whose ultimate source is God. *Barakah* is an intangible quality which enhances life in a variety of ways. Places like Mecca and Medina have this quality, so prayers performed in them are rewarded manyfold. Food that has *barakah* feeds more people than appears possible at first sight. One always wishes another's home, children or even vehicle God's bounteous *barakah* to sustain them with peace and tranquillity or trouble-free performance. Individuals who exude *barakah* are thought to be focal points of God's grace. Merely sitting in their company grants one access to this effulgence. Seeking the *barakah* of a saint may extend to using or even drinking the water that falls as he performs ablution. The saint, living or passed away, exudes this *barakah*, which then becomes the basis of a Sufi order or strong mobilization force. In this regard, the leadership type exemplified by the Shi'ite Imām may be seen as the archetype of the Sufi saint. The direct descendent of the most blessed person for all times becomes a model for other saints, who are similarly blessed. Both exemplify leadership through their personalities filled with *barakah* from God.

The leadership of the Sufis became almost legendary in North and West Africa in the eighteenth and nineteenth centuries. This had happened earlier as well, even though Sufis would not regard political power as their truest vocation. However, when political authority becomes weak and divisive, and the external pressures against Islamic society increase, then Sufi orders regard it as their responsibility to take over the mantle of political leadership. In the wake of internal decay and colonial pressure in the eighteenth and nineteenth centuries, numerous Sufi orders in parts of the Islamic world emerged to establish order and found polities around the *barakah* of saints and their descendents. Thus, the Sanūsiyyah in present-day Libya established a series of lodges in the southern reaches of the Sahara. These Sufi lodges provided religious guidance but also avenues for the regulation of social and political relations. The Sufi leaders became the mediators in conflict and provided the social structure for a highly mobile and sometimes volatile existence (Evans-Pritchard 1949).

Following full political control by European powers, other orders emerged to provide a sense of belonging in a world now dominated by European colonial powers. Some, like the Khatmiyyah and the Mouridiyyeh in Sudan and the Senegal respectively, thrived in a period of political powerlessness. They established cordial relations with Britain and France respectively and ensured their autonomy within their now restricted areas of jurisdiction. Following the demise of their founder, Ahmad Bamba (1850–1927), the Mouridiyyeh in Senegal built an economic empire on peanut production. The followers of the order were encouraged to desist from civil unrest, work hard and seek the blessings of the successors (*khalifah*s). The order was at once extremely co-operative with the colonial state and, at the same time, created a bulwark against its cultural influence. The Khatmiyyah established a similar relationship with the British during their authority over the Sudan. In each of these cases, the leadership of the order was justified and thrived on the reputation of being the spiritual location of the founder or his *khalīfah*s.

LEADERSHIP OF KNOWLEDGE

We now move on to another, equally prominent form of leadership in Islam. But first, we trace its roots to the early conflict in Islam. Those who preferred to stay out of the conflict altogether supported neither Ibn al-Zubayr nor Ḥusayn. In principle, these individuals in Medina did not even support the Umayyads. However, as so often happens in times of conflict, all choices became implicated: even those who refused to take sides supported one or the other group in spite of themselves. In such situations neutral positions become particularly untenable, even as they appear to be the only safe approaches. In the case of early Islam, as in many other conflicts, some scholars did try to maintain neutrality. The example of the legal scholar, Abū Ḥanīfah, discussed in Chapter 2, was a classic case of someone who refused to participate in the affairs of the state.

Abū Ḥanīfah was in fact unusual in his explicit rejection of the state and his refusal to take up a career in it. The silence of other scholars was at least implicit support for the status quo of the Umayyads. Many even took on bureaucratic positions as judges in the victorious states, and sometimes became tutors to their princes. If we take the example of Abū Ḥanīfah again, we find Ibn Abī Laylā (d. 765), also a prominent scholar in the city, taking a different political position. While Abū Ḥanīfah developed his legal authority within a circle of students, Ibn Abī Laylā worked from the demands of the state. The independent jurist and the court jurist were always potentially, if not actually, at loggerheads with each other. Abū Ḥanīfah's political stance, however, did not even become the norm of his school. His illustrious students served the Abbasid state as judges. It was the great fortune of al-Shāfi'ī that one them intervened on his behalf when he was brought as a rebel to the Abbasid court. Similarly, the great *ḥadīth* scholar al-Zuhrī was a judge and tutor closely associated with the Umayyad court. In this way, although the scholars tried to maintain neutrality in the face of revolts, their social positions were closely connected to the ruling class. Even their neutrality and silence became a support for the most effective and, thus, the most powerful. In political terms, this was the genesis of the Sunni approach to political power in Islam, and their model of leadership in Islamic society.

Political acquiescence provided a different kind of leadership model for society. On the surface, and in many specific contexts, the Sunni political position translated into servile acceptance of the status quo. But this kind of leadership was a bit more complex than appears at first sight. Many of these scholars regarded political power as inherently tainted, even as they sometimes co-operated with the state, and so we have to dig deeper to find out what was really going on. The careers of the early founders of jurisprudence bear testimony to this ambiguous position. Theirs was not an outright rejection of the court, but a desire to remain as far from it as possible. The great Ibn al-'Arabī advised his postulants 'not to frequent the doors of people in authority, nor keep company with those who covet worldly things' (quoted in Jeffreys 1962: 647). For scholars, in fact, true leadership belonged to those who engaged in a study of the texts and attained thereby a high degree of piety. The *'ulamā'*, literally 'those who have knowledge', exemplified this kind of leadership. They were, as stated in a well-known and much-quoted statement attributed to the Prophet, his true successors:

> The *'ulamā'* are the inheritors of the Prophets who bequeath knowledge. Whoever takes this, has received much and whoever goes on a trip seeking knowledge, God will make the road to paradise that much easier.
>
> (Ibn Ḥajr n. d.: I, 160)

This is the opening statement in Bukhārī's collection of *ḥadīth* on the value and eminence of knowledge in Islam. In this particular statement lies a distinct claim that knowledge (*'ilm*), and not *barakah* or blood relationship, was the basis of leadership. Whoever the ruler or leader might be at a particular instant, the *'ulamā'* determined the duties and responsibilities of the office of leadership.

Viewed from the perspective of knowledge as authority, we must take another look at the scholars. When the Umayyads first consolidated their power against both the Shi'ites and Ibn al-Zubayr, the scholars chose neutrality. However, towards the end of Umayyad rule, the scholarly circles engaged in the pursuit of knowledge became critical of the moral standards, or lack of them, displayed by the courts. They implicitly, and in many cases explicitly, supported the revolutionary opposition that gathered against the Umayyads.

In 750, a revolution witnessed the passing of leadership to the family of the Prophet, the descendants of al-'Abbās, an uncle of the Prophet. The Abbasids had gained the support of the Shi'ites, as well as the scholars. After the revolution, though, the caliphs desired absolute control and set about dismantling the power first of the Shi'ites and then of the *'ulamā'*. The Abbasid caliphs tried to eliminate all possible Shi'ite claimants to leadership. The most formidable in terms of symbolic power arose in Medina with Muḥammad b. 'Abd Allah al-Nafs al-Zakiyyah (d. 762–3) who gained support from a cross-section of Muslims. When the Abbasid armies marched to Medina, he defended the city in exactly the same manner as the Prophet Muhammad had defended it against an alliance launched by the Quraysh. Then, after presenting the matter for deliberation, the Prophet and his Companions had dug a trench on the vulnerable side of the city. Al-Nafs al-Zakiyyah followed this exact strategy against the Abbasid army. In his hands, though, the Prophetic strategy became a symbol of the Prophetic way. In this tragic defence of the city, al-Nafs al-Zakiyyah was following the exact *sunnah* of the Prophet, in accordance with the values that scholars had developed. Of course, the Abbasid army had no scruples regarding these symbols and values and crushed the revolt without compunction. Al-Nafs al-Zakiyyah's head was savagely severed and sent to Abū Ja'far (the second Abbasid caliph). The scholars proved easy to defeat in military terms, but they too, like the Shi'ites, survived long after the mighty Abbasids were gone.

The power of leadership based on knowledge emerged clearly when the Abbasids thought that they had consolidated their power and authority. The seventh Abbasid caliph, Ma'mūn, declared that all scholars should accept the doctrine of the createdness of the Qur'ān, and not dare to hold an opposing view. He instituted a formal *miḥnah* (inquisition) to enforce this doctrine among the prominent scholars of Islam. The Mu‘tazilites were the sponsors of this doctrine which argued that the Qur’ān, while still the word of God, should be regarded as a creation of God. Doctrinally, the Mu‘tazilites were engaged in debate with Christian theologians and Hellenistic philosophers who pointed out that the Word of God, in the form of the Qur’ān, could not be reconciled to the absolute unity that was claimed for God in Islam. Like the Logos in Christianity, the Islamic notion of the Qur’ān as the word of God compromised the unity of God. Politically speaking, however, the order of the caliph was an opportunity to harness and control the power of scholars who had been so effective in mobilizing public opinion against the Umayyads. The acceptance of a theological decree as determined by a caliph tested the nature of ultimate authority in society. If the caliphs were able to determine doctrine, scholars would be made subservient to power. Some scholars accepted the state's decree, but a small group resisted its interference in the determination of doctrine.

Aḥmad b. Ḥanbal (780–855), the leading jurist and *ḥadīth* scholar, became the most prominent symbol of the resistance to caliphal pressure. Ibn Ḥanbal's grandfather was one of the early Abbasid propagandists against the Umayyads, but he himself chose a scholarly career, living off a modest estate left by his father. Ma’mūn summoned him to his court, but died before Ibn Ḥanbal was brought to trial. The later Abbasid caliphs, particularly al-Mu‘taṣim, continued the inquisition and had Ibn Ḥanbal jailed for two years. Even in the face of imprisonment and torture he refused to accept the ruling doctrine. In principle, he refused to accept that theological scholastics could be applied in order to understand the nature of God. In reference to such questions, Ibn Ḥanbal simply insisted on repeating the relevant Qur’ānic text. He was eventually released and then withdrew from public life. When he was invited to the court after the inquisition had been ended, he still chose not to be involved. Ibn Ḥanbal's work spanned both the collection of *ḥadīth* and jurisprudence. His sons, Ṣāliḥ and ‘Abd Allāh, continued his tradition in both areas. Ṣāliḥ, transmitting his jurisprudence, became a judge in Isfahan in present-day Iran, while ‘Abd Allāh established his legacy as a jurist and *ḥadīth* scholar. For the purpose of our discussion of leadership, Ibn Ḥanbal's position on the Qur’ān had far-reaching implications for the relationship between political power and scholarship. The inability of the caliph to bring about consensus around a doctrinal issue, either by persuasion or force, meant that scholarship prevailed, if not triumphed, over brute power. It was not a complete victory, as witnessed by the fact that one of Ibn Ḥanbal's sons became a judge for the Abbasid empire. On the other hand, Ibn Ḥanbal's resistance meant that the authority of the scholars was firmly entrenched. While their independence was not guaranteed, their authority could not be ignored. The determination of legal and theological matters of religion was the preserve of the scholars. It was they who would henceforth advise the ruling authorities.

Of course, this theoretical priority of knowledge over power could not be maintained. Sunni scholars often depended for their stipends and jobs on courts established by the state. Most tried to be independent, like Abū Ḥanīfah and Ibn Ḥanbal, but many took up positions in the state. The ideal engagement of jurisprudence and theology was an avoidance of the messy world of political power. Scholars were content to specify certain minimum requirements that political authorities had to maintain. Among these were the implementation of Islamic law through a judicial system and the protection of the borders. As a result, they often tolerated oppressive rulers and implicitly gave their stamp of approval to the machinations of brute force.

And yet they wielded considerable symbolic power in the cities of Islam. With the support of pious endowments that built mosques and schools, the scholars were able to create religious communities within the larger structures of the state. The endowments were established by wealthy individuals, political patrons and traders. Islamic legal doctrines ensured, to a certain extent, that the endowments came with few strings attached. Those who wished to make pious endowments had to accept the rules of the game as determined by scholarly religious criteria. In his fascinating study of the Islamic cities before the rise of the Ottomans in the fifteenth century, Lapidus pointed to the important role played by the scholars. They came from a vast range of classes, and were the truly integrated and representative group in a diverse cosmopolitan society. While they themselves did not wield power, they determined the 'patterns of social activity and organisation which served to create a more broadly based community' (Lapidus 1967: 107). Jurisprudence and theology determined the norms and boundaries of these communities, led by recognizable schools and recognizable personalities.

Within Sunnism, four schools of jurisprudence determined the distinct boundaries of these communities. These were the Ḥanafīs (traced back to Abū Ḥanīfah), the Mālikīs (from Anas b. Mālik), the Ḥanbalīs (from

Aḥmad b. Ḥanbal) and the Shāfi'īs (from Muḥammad b. Idrīs al-Shāfi'ī). Each of these schools developed a body of jurisprudence, a methodology, a lineage of succession to their founder and a clear identity within the larger Muslim community. The schools were often region-specific, like the Mālikīs in North Africa and the Ḥanafīs in India. Sometimes, though, they lived side by side. The following observation by Ibn Baṭṭūṭah about the various schools in Mecca illustrates the distinct identity they cultivated and by implication, the authority of the jurists who led them:

> during the week, the first of the four *imams* to recite the daily prayer is the Shafi'i imam. The majority of the Meccans belong to this rite and he is appointed by those in authority . . . When the Shafi'i imam has finished his prayer, the imam of the Malikites prays in a separate oratory facing the Ka'ba's southern angle; the imam of the Hanbalites prays along with him facing the eastern wall of the shrine. Lastly, the Hanafi imam prays, facing the roof spout of the shrine . . . this order of the prayer remains the same for four of the five daily prayers. At the sunset prayer they pray in unison, each imam leading his own congregation.
>
> (quoted in Wolfe 1997: 64)

Such an organization of worship performed within one space may be seen as an inspiring illustration of pluralism within Islam at its best. Each school led a congregation and agreed to disagree. On the other hand, it graphically depicts the communal boundaries drawn by the schools among Muslims as a whole. The legal schools became the key inter-Muslim identities in the great and vast world of Islam. They determined and located the social and religious boundaries and values of religious communities.

From a social point of view, the urban Sufi orders performed a similar task of determining order, morality and ultimate authority. The tomb of 'Ā'ishah al-Mannūbiyyah in Tunis is a typical example. She was 'Ā'ishah b. 'Īmrān al-Ḥajj (d. *c.* 1257) from a village called Mannūbah near Tunis. She refused to marry her cousin and arrived in Tunis, settling near its gates among the marginalized peoples of the city. Many miracles are attributed to her. Even today, both girls and boys in Tunis are named Manūbi after her. In addition, she is also reputed to have been the student of the great Sufi al-Shādhilī (1196–1258). Both during her life and afterwards, through the Sufi order that grew up around her, 'Ā'ishah al-Mannūbiyyah provided a sense of belonging and identity to people living in a large and inhospitable city. Like the legal schools, the urban Sufi orders created religious identities and communities around a set of teachings, values, practices and symbols. In some way, both saints and scholars created quasi-political identities apart from the larger political entities of caliphates and sultanates.

During the Ottoman period, the scholars were able to take the arrangement between religious identity and political power one step further, by gaining the support of the Janissary military troops. Unlike the earlier scholarly communities, the Ottoman Shaykh al-Islam was appointed by the Sultan and supported by groups within the military establishment. When the Ottomans wished to introduce reforms in the nineteenth century, the scholars, with the support of the troops, resisted these reforms. Both realized the erosion of their influence that would follow from the proposed reforms. However, unlike the earlier scholars, the Ottoman religious hierarchy enjoyed a permanent place in the state, with good military support. Only with the disbanding of the troops in 1826, and thereby the elimination of the power of the scholars, was Mahmud II able to pave the way for reforms (Voll 1982: 90–1). The example of the Ottoman period does not disprove the general rule that the scholars were able to create sub-communities within which they wielded considerable moral power. The additional military power, and its subsequent loss, merely highlights the dominant model. And this model establishes the authority of knowledge that regulates personal life, and plays a careful balancing act with brute power.

The model of leadership founded on knowledge and religious stature was not exclusive to Sunni circles. It is also true of the Twelver Shiʿite scholars after the concealment, or occultation, of the twelfth Imām. This group, representing the majority of Shiʿites, believe that the twelfth Imām, Muḥammad al-Muntaẓar, had gone into concealment in 873 and was then represented by his deputies until 940 (Hodgson 1974: I, 377). Following this period of 'lesser occultation', jurists and theologians took on the guardianship of the community in the name of the Imām. The concept of the guardianship of the jurists (*wilāyat al-faqīh*) in Shiʿism resembles the role of Sunni scholars as the inheritors of the prophets. In both cases, the scholars determine the moral and spiritual limits of a community. The example of the Shiʿite Imāms, in fact, highlights the greater potential inherent in the Sunni case. In the former, the scholars also collected the taxes due to the family of the Prophet. With this financial base, generally missing in the Sunni case, the scholars have been able to build a scholarly infrastructure of mosques, schools and lodges which is the envy of any religious order. In the twentieth century, Ayatollah Khomeini appealed to this concept of the guardianship of the jurists in order to lead the Islamic revolution in the name of the last Imām.

Thus the scholars turned their attention to the transmission, preservation and explication of the records of the past. They were the principal expositors of the values of Islam as belief and practice. From the Qur'ān to the Prophetic biographies to jurisprudence, these scholars, particularly those who chose to remain out of the political contest on principle or in preparation for the Imām, were the first to establish the scholarly disciplines within Islam. With them, writing and literacy of the sacred texts became a ground for authority within society. In contrast to the power of the political leaders and the charismatic personalities of the Imāms and Sufi leaders, the prestige of the scholars lay in their literacy and scholarship. Their leadership was recognized and respected because they were the bearers of the texts of Islam. In this way, they laid the foundation for a specific form of authority within Islam. Distinct from the powerful commanders on the battlefield as well as from the personal models of piety, these scholars based their authority on knowledge of the textual disciplines. Knowledge of the text became a distinctive criterion of leadership in Islamic history.

LEADERSHIP BEYOND MODELS

Islamic leadership comes in three distinct models. The political rulers claimed leadership on the basis of their succession to the Prophet and their possession of power. The Umayyads even dared to experiment with a mandate from God. This authority based on power was tempered and challenged by other forms of authority. The Shi'ites proposed a leadership of exemplary personalities, while Sunni leadership rested on access to textual support. These 'ideal types' of Islamic leadership appear to have eclipsed the ambiguity of leadership quoted in 'Umar's statement at the head of this chapter. Leadership of text, prophetic ancestry and political power admit no doubt and no ambiguity. They certainly seem to push into the background the egalitarian and radical non-elitism in 'Umar's statement. The foregoing, it must be born in mind, are only models of leadership. They should not replace the actual leaders of Islamic society. When we look at Islam in actual practice, power, personal charisma and textual acumen intermesh with each other in interesting ways.

The discussion of leadership would not be complete without touching on some of the iconoclastic traits within Islamic leadership expectations. While authorities are recognized in Islam, their powers are limited by certain characteristics within Islam and Islamic societies. The first of these is the notion that there is no priesthood in Islam. Numerous scholars have noted the absence of an establishment that represents the voice of official Islam. Modern Muslim apologetic is particularly proud to celebrate this very modern concept of religion in which the individual's faith is not mediated through officially sanctioned religious structures. In this regard, Islam is more like Protestantism than Catholicism. Like the former, Muslims do not require the structure and efficacy of a specially consecrated class of men or women to attain salvation. Islam even takes Protestantism one step further, by completely eliminating sacraments and the very notion of ordination.

Unfortunately, considerable confusion exists both within and outside Islam about this element. It is certainly true that there is no religiously established clergy in Islam. However, this does not mean that Islam does not have channels through which God can be reached. Text, disciplines and charismatic individuals, as I have already outlined, have played this role in the past and continue to do so in the present. Individuals and groups claim to lead Muslims to God, guaranteeing this passage through their access to text, their exemplary character or by virtue of their close proximity to the model of the Prophet. These channels have founded leadership patterns in Muslim society, and the institutional structure of Muslim society certainly suggests a de facto clergy if not a clergy confirmed by teachings in Islam.

But this is where the ambiguity of leadership shines through. The absence of priesthood means the absence of what Nasr calls a focus and centre in the tradition:

> Islam is not a 'centered' religion to the degree that Christianity is. Where the latter provides imagery of center, pivot, and focus, these fitting Christ perfectly, Islam is like a block. Or to change metaphors, if Christianity is like a centering fire, Islam is like a sheet of snow. Importance adheres to its totality, through which it spreads more or less evenly, unifying and leveling concomitantly.
>
> (Nasr 1994: ix)

In its leadership dimension, this lack of centre implies that leadership within Islam remains open. No central authority exists to confer legitimacy. If anything, authority truly rests on the acceptance of the group which leaders claim to lead.

A fascinating example of this de-centering of authority comes from a village in Madascar studied by Paul Lambek. Here, the local imāms are chosen by virtue of their expertise and knowledge of the Qur'ān and other central texts in Islam. However, since the villagers are ignorant of Arabic, they judge the preachers on the basis of non-textual criteria. In particular, Lambek recounts one of the ways in which the preacher's fidelity to the values and the teachings in the Qur'ān is judged. A preacher must ascend the *minbar*, which is covered with a very slippery carpet. If he slips by stepping carelessly onto the *minbar*, then he is suspected of some Qur'ānic moral failing. In this case, leadership cannot be taken lightly. It certainly cannot be taken as a given rank within the community simply on the basis of knowing the texts. One has to also exemplify the virtues of the text, as conceptualized by the villagers. As Lambek concludes, this means that knowledge itself is not a guarantor of a leadership position; 'personal behaviour must be seen to accord with the purity of the knowledge [a leader] invokes' (Lambek 1990: 30).

This particular approach to leadership is also revealed in the nature of mystical experience and accomplishment in Islam. In Sufism, numerous attempts have been made to specify the various states of consciousness an adept must pass through in order to draw near to God. Moreover, numerous claims have been made that a particular individual has reached a level of spiritual accomplishment. In spite of these, however, individual achievement seems to elude the Muslim mystic. Andrae suggests that this is possibly related to 'the powerful sense of God's activity' in Islam (Andrae 1987: 81). It seems to me that this insecurity is clearly related to the deeply felt precarious position that such a visionary may achieve in Islam. When all believers are brothers and sisters, how dare one claim for oneself a degree above another? Massignon highlighted a similar concern to deal with what he calls 'the sciences of the heart' among al-Ḥallāj's contemporaries. The Mu'tazilites sought to include the basis of inner states of being as a rational endeavour, as opposed to the Sunnis, who left it to the grace of God. The latter rightly declared that such inner dimensions of a person's being were not open to scrutiny. According to Massignon, however, al-Ḥallāj's attitude, which permeated his entire life, was that the inner being of a person must continuously respond to the call of God, and never rest (Massignon 1982: 25). This restlessness and insecurity, in spite of their high spiritual accomplishments, has always instilled a deep sense of humility in mystics. From a perspective of leadership in Islam, this notion must indeed recall 'Umar's warning to his governor: 'Is it not sufficient that you are standing while the people are sitting?' This precarious notion of leadership is also captured in the Qur'ān: 'most noble of you are the most God-conscious [possessing *taqwā*]' (49:13). A Prophetic statement reminds the scholars that they may be among the first to enter hellfire. By a dramatic inversion of what seems to be expected, both verse and statement alert us to the fragility of leadership. Thus the principle that there may be no central religious hierarchy in Islam means that leadership is extremely fragile and not conferred with any degree of finality. It does not mean that models of authority are completely absent in Islam.

Our discussion of the particular position of the *imām* in the mosque highlighted the presence of leadership in Islam. I began with the ambiguity and precariousness of leadership, but then proceeded to outline the leadership models that have emerged in the history of Islam. Following the example of the Prophet, political leadership has always been a central feature of the faith. Sometimes, this has translated into the leadership of the powerful. On the other hand, personal exemplification of values has been manifested within Shi'ism and Sufism. Here, leadership and authority inheres within the persons involved. Finally, the importance of knowledge and texts has assured some authority to the *'ulamā'*. These three ideal models of leadership intermesh in actual Muslim contexts. Historical models do not guarantee leadership, they only discover patterns in reality. In Muslim contexts, leadership remains a restless, dangerous venture, even as it promises much.

6 CHALLENGES AND OPPORTUNITIES IN THE TWENTY-FIRST CENTURY

In this short introduction, my exploration of the symbols, values and images of Islam has been guided by the physical and conceptual features of the mosque. I want to change course in this final chapter, focus on the state of the Muslims at the end of the twentieth century and the eve of the twenty-first. This chapter paints a general picture of the key challenges and opportunities, the hopes and fears facing Islam and Muslims. Colonialism, modernity and globalization have presented Muslims with a great number of challenges. Whether in matters of beliefs, worldviews or practices, these global historical forces have forced Muslims to adapt and grapple with their traditions. Some of these forces have caused extreme tensions within the house of Islam. Colonialism and Western hegemony led to the great destruction of communities, regions and psychological wellbeing. Not all contemporary changes have been negative, though. Modern transport, for example, has greatly improved the capacity to perform the annual pilgrimage, and modern media have created opportunities for a greater sense of the international *ummah* than ever before. The end of the twentieth century thus presents an opportunity to risk some general comments around the themes of globalization, human rights and religious values.

GLOBALIZATION

The desire to get from one place to another may be thought of as a challenge, and all forms of transport and communication may be thought of as means to overcome the challenge. As we find quicker ways of getting from one point to another, we literally and figuratively reduce the challenge. The use of the donkey, the horse, the wheel and the internal combustion engine each, in its revolutionary way, overcame these challenges and reduced the distance from one point to another. Through the revolutionary means of communication of more recent times, we realize that we live in a global village. Television brings us images, both positive and negative, of events taking place halfway around the world or halfway around the solar system. Telephone networks put us in touch with people and the Internet bombards us with an incessant stream of data. In the past ten years the use of computer communications has brought home the realization that something is constantly happening, somewhere, with a force felt by almost every person on the globe.

The question that concerns me here is the impact that the global village has on Islam. Islam, like all religions and cultures, presents a mind map of the world we live in. Its geography boasts of Mecca at the centre of the world, even the universe, and its legal discourse determines what is far and what is not. For example, if a Muslim leaves his or her home on a journey that would a take a fully laden camel a day and night of normal walking, then that person should shorten the compulsory prayers. The rules of shortening prayers in Islam are more complex than this, but the point being made here is that a certain form of transport shapes the idea of distance. What happens when the camel, even in Saudi Arabia, can only be seen in a zoo, and is replaced by cars and jets? Does the religious legal tradition have to revise its expectations of worshippers, by converting the distance travelled into kilometres or miles? Or should it rethink the meaning of travel itself? This simple example represents only the tip of the iceberg of problems, questions and challenges that face a historical tradition shaped and formulated in a world that was much larger and slower than the one we live in at the end of twentieth century. This chapter is concerned with raising such global issues.

It was once thought progressive communication and globalization would progressively reduce the viability of traditional religions and cultures. As we now know, this has not happened. Globalization at the end of the twentieth century has shattered one of the powerful myths of the modern world: the belief and hope in the progressive secularization of the world. This worldly mission dominated the theme of journalists, social scientists and politicians until the late 1970s and deserves some clarification. The first wave of modern globalization began with the power of steam, gunpowder and the musket to conquer vast territories and peoples. The colonization of the rest of the world by small countries in Europe was a devastating form of globalization. However, at this stage, globalization was a form of Europeanization, and its overwhelming outlook was a belief in the progressive demystification and naturalization of the world. This outlook was driven by an overriding optimism in the reliability of science and the power of the human spirit to overcome all obstacles. The faith in science celebrated its ability to understand nature and put it to practical use for the happiness of humankind; the belief in the human spirit was the realization that humankind was on its own because the gods were either non-existent, retired, uninterested or simply dead. Science and humanism were two powerful waves that would sweep away all superstitions, magic and primitive religions from the world. Religion, if it survived, would be benign, an 'alternative culture, observed as unthreatening to the modern social system, in much the same way that entertainment is seen as unthreatening' (Wilson 1985: 20). It was believed that once more people appreciated the two powers of science and the human spirit, the natural and inexorable outcome would be peace and happiness for all. Science and the human spirit could not be resisted as, sooner or later, they triumphed over all previous conceptualizations of the world. This was the crude form of secularization theory.

Of course, this did not happen. Recent trends in world politics and globalization have brought home that truth in unmistakable ways. Science understood a great deal of what was taking place in nature, but could not service everybody's happiness. It was too expensive, and its advantages were more accessible to those who could afford its costs. While science has no doubt benefited everybody on the planet in one way or another, its benefit for the rich has far outweighed its benefit for the poor. Moreover, the pursuit of science and its utilization in war, industry and leisure has produced a great number of unintended consequences: uneven development, destructive bombs, waste problems and the extinction of plant and animal species. While the modern venture has ensured abundance and prosperity for some and a steady trickle of benefits for the rest, it has also displayed the human propensity to evil, sowing moral destruction and ethical emptiness. Freedom has produced brilliant creativity, but also left a trail of corruption, greed and depravity not unlike that exhibited in the name of gods or kings.

It is in such a world that religion, culture and values have begun to reassert their prestige and power. Religion, in particular, has been used by individuals to find psychological solace because it 'offers another world to explore as an escape from the rigors of technological order and the ennui that is the incidental by-product of an increasingly programmed world' (Wilson 1985: 20). The search for spirituality across the whole world, but more emphatically in the highly developed world, turns increasingly to religion and religious practices. A new spirituality is found at the core of human life. But in the modern world, religion is not only the preserve of highly industrialized boredom. Religion is also the foundation of strong group identities either expressing the sigh of the oppressed as Marx characterized, or providing the power and identity to stake a claim in social and political struggles. In this regard, religion is sometimes inextricably linked to ethnic or linguistic groups who make a bid for greater political and social power. The breakup of the Soviet empire has revealed the power of Islam to galvanize and mobilize its Turkish- and Persian-speaking peoples. Ethnicity and Muslim identity also converge, and sometimes compete with other political tendencies, in China, Pakistan, Bosnia, the Philippines, Malaysia, Khurdistan and, last but not least, among the Arabs themselves (Eickelman and Piscatori 1996: 99–107). Also, it must be said that religion provides an opportunity to forge a larger group by bringing together small fragmented identities. This is clearly evident of Islam in America and in other minority contexts. Both as the cement that glues groups together and the force that gives new meaning to ethnic or linguistic identity, religion in general, and Islam in particular, returns to the centre stage of public life at the end of the twentieth century. Against the prediction of crude secularization, religion claims its place in the public sphere as both spiritual quest and group identity.

A closer look at these recent developments has generated two competing theories among social scientists. The first, advocated by Huntingdon, is a recognition of the deep differences in the world: 'Culture and cultural identities, which at the broadest level are civilisation identities, are shaping the patterns of cohesion, disintegration, and conflict in the post-Cold War period' (Huntingdon 1996: 20). According to this view, the world must be understood as distinct cultural–civilization zones which have a very different way of looking at reality. The failure to recognize these differences will lead to disasters in understanding and dealing with conflicts and strife. Addressed primarily to American foreign-policymakers, Huntingdon's thesis advised the United States State Department to change its perception of the world in order to cope better with preserving and extending American interests.

For our purposes, it is important to note that Huntingdon regarded Islam as the foundation of a unique civilization. This is an understanding of Islam that coincides with what some Muslims are increasingly advocating. Islamic political activists, particularly, have been insisting that the social and political system of Islam should be the source and foundation of state, judicial and educational systems. Islam determines everything in Muslim societies, at the very least affecting how people do business, worship, greet and fight with each other. It would seem that some Muslim groups clearly confirm Huntingdon's analysis. Militant groups in various parts of the world draw definite boundaries around an Islamic identity and resist the encroachment of secularism and Western influence. This has become a common phenomenon in the anti-Americanism that sweeps Muslim communities. Certain groups openly advocate military *jihād*, both against their own governments and against the West in general. In our first scenario of Muslims at the end of twentieth century, therefore, we have mutual antagonism between Muslims and the Other.

Other observers take great exception to Huntingdon's analysis, and to those Muslims who fail to recognize important changes in the practice of Islam in the global village. Both Huntingdon and radical Islamists confirm each other's fears and prejudices as they fail to take note of cultural developments in a global world. This is evident, at one level, in the extent to which Muslim share in the global consumer culture. The diversity of religions and cultures belies the homogeneity that lies under the surface of globalization. The world has shrunk, most of all in relation to the spread of consumer commodities to every corner of the globe. Thus, in spite of the rise of religious and cultural identities, we are witnessing the homogenization of culture around brand names churned out by multinational companies with financial centres in one part of the world, sweatshop factories in another, and consumers in yet another. Underneath the diversity of cultures lies the greater uniformity of a Coca-Cola culture that unites all humankind in one family. Only those religious tendencies that embrace and adopt Coca-Cola by, for example, adding a *ḥalāl* sign on its side, indicating that it is fit for Muslim consumption, are coping and thriving in the global world. They give in to the spread of Coca-Colization but also ensure their place in the twenty-first century. In spite of the fiery rhetoric, then, there seems to be a transformation of religious practices almost imperceptible to those who belong to a particular tradition.

In addition to the shared base of consumer culture, developments within Islam and Muslim communities also shatter the myth of the continuity of Islamic culture as a unique and unchanging civilization pitted against the outside world. Muslim people, like everybody else in the global village, are continuously moving and making homes in parts of the world that were previously considered culturally homogeneous. Immigrant Muslims in Europe and North America are forcing the host communities to rethink the relation of religion and society, religion and public symbols. The scarf issue in secular European societies is symptomatic of this shift. Deep prejudices are coming to the fore, as different perceptions of religion and public life collide. At the same time, Muslims themselves are grappling with the challenges of being Muslim in new social and political contexts. Some Muslims are turning to religion even if they were not previously very religious in their home countries, a change sometimes forced by questions of identity and marginalization. And so they turn to a tradition and expect it to provide something new for them. For example, the minority status of Muslims in secular or Christian-dominated societies is a mirror image of the *dhimmī* (protected) status of minority religions in early Islamic empires. However, modern notions of democracy, minority rights and cultural pride provide new opportunities previously denied to minorities anywhere. If, in its best application, the *dhimmī* system granted rights to minority religion unmatched at the time, it cannot stand the test of democratic rights without modification and development. Consequently, European and North American Muslims have to shape Islamic values with very little assistance from traditional models. Some of the deep differences among Muslims in their new contexts are symptomatic of their having to shape Islamic values in open, democratic, multicultural societies.

The adaptation of Islam to globalization is not a phenomenon peculiar to the end of the twentieth century, the radical responses of Islamist groups or immigrant Muslims. Globalization has penetrated deep into the fibre of being Muslim. I shall discuss one feature that illustrates the nature and impact of this penetration. As the world became progressively smaller, it brought together Muslims from a variety of backgrounds and schools. Thus it is not surprising to note that at the turn of the nineteenth century reformists like Muḥammad Abduh advocated the doctrine of *talfīq* in Islamic jurisprudence. Contrary to traditional practice, Abduh and his followers advocated that one could justifiably follow the judgement of any recognized school of thought. The word *talfīq* means the act of patching a garment with a variety of pieces. It was previously frowned upon as an arbitrary and opportunistic legal practice. However, the reformist advocated it as a means of overcoming legal problems in one school by turning to more appropriate answers in another. As Muslims moved into the twentieth century, the option was followed by others who were at one time intractable foes of *talfīq*. Masud studied the views of traditional scholars in India who had employed it to address the problem of abused women in the first half of the century. According to Ḥanafī jurisprudence, which most Indians followed, women could not initiate divorce proceedings for any reason whatsover. Many abused women realized, however, that if they declared themselves apostates, their terrible marriages would be automatically annulled. At first the staunch Ḥanafī jurists of India refused to consider the challenge, but later opted to assist abused women by allowing them redress through Mālikī jurisprudence. This was an example of *talfīq* employed by reputable jurists who, in other respects, continued to advocate the strict adherence to one single legal school (Masud 1996).

Certainly, jurists were aware of the provisions of the different legal schools in pre-modern times. However, contact between peoples, and not only between scholars, was previously minimal and scholars belonged to schools and orders from which it was difficult to distance oneself. With greater access to modern transportation, the semi-secluded state of the Muslim peoples progressively decreased, and the possibilities of different and competing legal schools could not be ignored. Even today, the pilgrimage to Mecca comes as a shock to many Muslims as far as the variation of ritual practices is concerned – and I not referring here to cultural practices, but to the religious obligations on which there is general consensus within Islam. In such a situation, therefore, the practice of *talfīq* becomes a strong argument against those who advocate fidelity to one legal school. For centuries, jurists have themselves said that all the legal schools are correct in their judgements: it does not make sense now to say that one may not follow their rulings. From solving legal problems, then, *talfīq* has now become a way of practising Islam. Numerous compendiums of practical *Sharī'ah* are written on this basis, and jurists give opinions (*fatwā*) assuming that it is the more magnanimous and accepted way of dealing with the issues challenging

Muslims at the end of twentieth century. The result, of course, is the patched frock of Islamic jurisprudence which traditional scholars decried. However, one cannot help noting that it is a garment that admirably suits late twentieth-century postmodern culture, which, while it may not consists entirely of continuous play, does have a tendency to accommodate diversity and difference to an extent impossible in one legal school.

The subtle change within Islamic practice, adjusting to Coca-Cola culture or adapting legal practice, is also evident among the militant, radical groups. In spite of the rejectionist rhetoric, even radical groups are affected and assisted by globalization. Even as they champion the return to an authentic Islam, they are not immune from its impact: to some extent, they even thrive on the possibilities it generates. Modern means of communication are employed to mobilize Muslims around issues and concerns. To the extent that global media communicate the joys and pains of Muslims around the globe, there is a greater sense and awareness of the *ummah*. This sentiment can be successfully marshalled in support of causes, real and imagined. But there are also costs for employing mass media. There is a greater tendency for Islam to be projected as an advertisement that can be packaged in manageable and effective thirty-second soundbites, stickers and pamphlets. Slogans replace beliefs and form takes precedence over substance. To this extent, Huntingdon's thesis of incompatible cultural groups and civilizations is belied: we do not get culturally incompatible groups and civilizations across the global village, but competing and antagonistic packages of modern culture. This is not to deny deep differences between Islamists and their antagonists, but rather to point to common ways of putting together cultural options in a global world.

No doubt globalization has had an impact on the particular practice and understanding of Islam. As elsewhere, religious values have returned to the public sphere in way that had not been envisaged after the Second World War. However, the return to religious values and traditions has not meant a return to tradition and an escape from the effect of globalization. Rather, the global village has demanded far-reaching changes in how Muslims practise religious law and how they think of Muslims elsewhere. Radical groups of Islamists who shout about returning to Islam are not excluded from this process. Aspects of globalization tinge the very form and substance of their re-Islamization.

HUMAN RIGHTS: SEEKING EQUITY IN A GLOBAL VILLAGE

Globalization has also placed religion, culture and human rights at the top of the agenda of world relations. One of the most enduring documents of the United Nations has been its charter of human rights, laying down a benchmark of the fundamental, inalienable rights of all human beings, irrespective of gender, colour, race, ethnicity, class or creed. At the founding of the United Nations in 1948 the question of the relation between religion and human rights could be ignored, because religion was thought of as a private matter. The fact that religion at the time was not a private affair for most people on the globe did not seem to bother many of the founders. Religion would eventually become a private affair under the impact of secularization. Of course this has not happened as predicted, and religion has returned to public life with confidence and power. No longer the preserve of private life, the question of religion and human rights can no longer be ignored.

Before I consider the question of human rights and Islam, I want briefly to look at the question of human rights in relation to religion in principle. Some scholars are of the opinion that the relation between religion and basic human rights is problematic, to say the least. Religion is concerned with the search for transforming the individual, and has not therefore been concerned about the inalienable worth of an individual. From a religious perspective, human beings are unbelievers, sinners, unfulfilled, unenlightened, or their opposites. This hierarchy at best obscured or ignored the underlying quality of human beings as human beings. In the light of this difficulty, the arbitrary invention of human rights within a particular culture will not endure political and social struggles. On the other hand, theistic religions have to contend with a concept of an ultimate being that controls and determines everything: the idea of human rights assumes an independent human being who is free to act and think. The metaphysical presence of transcendental being can only deny such a right at a fundamental level. On the positive side, it may be possible to say that the compassionate aspect of religious practice may serve a useful function in support of those whose rights are denied. It cannot in principle grant such rights to all human beings (Kinghorn 1991; Clasquin 1993; Prozesky 1989; Moosa 1991).

Against these misgivings, there are also those who believe that religion can provide the basis of a human rights culture. The twentieth century provides opportunities for religions to unearth their inherent values. For all the differences and boundaries established by religious traditions, religions can be described 'as ways of experimenting in being human' (Chidester 1992: xiii). Religions are thus not static and timeless, but can be modified and adapted to a global human rights culture. Some may object to this guarded and conditional congruence between religion and human rights. For some the idea of religion being adapted to a social context smacks of opportunism, which religion has always resisted. Religion is eternal and enduring, and a compromise or modification would undermine its very basis. This is a legitimate concern and may be addressed by pointing out the fundamental difference between opportunism in the service of selfish interests, and the demands of human rights. The first concerns the careful manner in which moral and religious values must be guarded against abuse. Thus, moral and virtuous conduct must be maintained against such abuse. The demands of human rights, on the other hand, try to uphold the freedom and dignity of individuals and societies. It is one of the greatest ironies of the modern period that religions have to defend themselves against the morality of human rights. Apart from this moral foundation of human rights, it cannot be denied that religion is continuously being transformed and adapted to historical contexts. The suspension of this transformation in the face of human rights would be the second irony, if it were not also tragic.

In the rest of the section, I want to explore such possibilities in relation to Islam. Islam, as a tradition and a system of values, possesses the necessary resources to justify and develop the concept of human rights. Such rights would be available to all individuals regardless of their race, colour, class, ethnic origin or belief system. A whole list of contemporary authorities may be marshalled to support this position, but it will suffice in this short introduction to Islam to present the salient arguments for such a position from Abdulaziz Sachedina. Such a presentation will explore the possibilities and the problems facing Muslims on this important question.

Sachedina deals particularly with the question of freedom of conscience, which is contentious for Muslims. When the UN Declaration of Human Rights was proclaimed in 1948, Saudi Arabia abstained from endorsing the freedom of conscience clause, refusing to accept it because it went against a statement attributed to the Prophet, that a person who leaves his religion should be killed (Little, Kelsay and Sachedina 1988: 35). At the time Pakistan argued for a completely different position that accorded with the liberal position of its reformist politicians. Clearly, this is an important principle of human rights, and one that cannot be left to difference of opinion pertaining to matters of detail in ritual practice. The Saudi position represents a literal fidelity to Islamic sources and challenges the possibility of human rights being endorsed by Islam. Pakistan, on the other hand, may be regarded as a deviation. Upon closer investigation, however, it turns out that the Saudi position may not necessarily be the authentic Islamic position.

Sachedina's argument for freedom of conscience, and by extension for all human rights in Islam, rests on three key points. First, he argues that the Qur'ān should be the basis for the development of a human rights culture within Islam. Other religious texts and subsequent Islamic history should be judged on the basis of the Qur'ān. Thus, for example, the particular history of early Islam or the collection of Prophetic statements should only be used in the light of the Qur'ān itself, and not to develop an ethic in conflict with its general argument. In a careful reading of the sacred text of Islam, Sachedina identifies in the Qur'ān 'an objective and universal moral nature on the basis of which all human beings are to be treated equally and held equally accountable to God'. Second, he finds that the Qur'ān posits that 'certain moral prescriptions follow from a common human nature and are regarded as independent of particular spiritual beliefs' (Little, Kelsay and Sachedina 1988: 62). The Qur'ān, according to Sachedina, insists that human beings are expected to acknowledge their inherent spirituality and moral nature. It appeals to human beings to find these basic truths on the basis of free choice. The following verse is a terse but eloquent testament to this fundamental essence: 'There is no compulsion in religion; truth stands out from error' (Qur'ān 3:256). Of course, it does not mean that the Qur'ān regards true religion as equivalent to falsehood, but Sachedina argues that the Qur'ān appeals to a basic human capacity inherent in all human beings to know and recognize truth, and it is on this foundation that a culture of human rights may be built: 'By recognising the capacity for universal righteousness that can be found among the adherents of other religious traditions, the Qur'ān sets forth a fundamental principle of religious liberty' (Little, Kelsay and Sachedina 1988: 76).

The third key to Sachedina's argument is the distinction between the moral rules and the religious rules and expectations imposed upon humankind in the Qur'ān. The moral injunctions of the Qur'ān pertain to the organization of a society in general, and they are applicable to all those who live in a society. In modern terms, this would include injunctions regarding murder, rape, treason, theft and the like. The religious injunctions, on the other hand, pertain only to matters of individual conscience. Thus, he argues that when the first caliph Abū Bakr launched the so-called apostasy campaigns shortly after the death of the Prophet, he was not forcing people to become Muslims. These campaigns were misnamed as *riddah* (apostasy) in later Islamic scholarship to nullify the freedom of conscience provided in the Qur'ān. In fact, Sachedina argued, in early post-Prophetic society 'apostasy infringes on private and community interests in the public order' (Little, Kelsay and Sachedina 1988: 76). Abū Bakr launched campaigns against the tribes because they withheld their *zakāh* (wealth-tax) and declared themselves independent of Medinan authority. These actions constituted a challenge to the legitimacy of the state, and were not simply acts of apostasy in the way we would understand the term today. Thus, if we make a distinction between the moral and the properly religious, the Qur'ān unconditionally supports freedom of conscience as far as the latter is concerned. The religious sphere is guided by deep personal conscience, while the moral guides the organization of society. Sachedina says that there is a dynamic tension in the Qur'ān between morality and religion that should not be missed in formulating policies on rights in a modern Islamic society or states.

Freedom of conscience, then, was founded on the innate disposition of all humans to recognize truth, the freedom to do so, and the distinction between moral and religious injunctions in the Qur'ān. This is a considerable advance on the Saudi reluctance to sign unconditionally the declaration of human rights. However, some problems still remain as far as finding a basis for a multicultural society at the end of the twentieth century is concerned. Assuming that one can adequately separate the moral from the religious, it is not so clear whether a multicultural society could be founded on the moral or the religious rules within Islam. It appears that early Islamic society was founded on the moral precepts of the Qur'ān, exactly those which conflict with the freedom of conscience clauses in the UN Declaration of Human Rights and which are thus inadequate for an inherently pluralistic world. Sachedina appears to be saying that freedom of conscience that is available to all must become the contemporary moral foundation of society, an analysis that implys a radical departure from traditional Islamic conceptions of a society. Founded on a modern interpretation of the Qur'ān, his insightful suggestions remain to be accepted by many Muslims.

Rather than a brilliant interpretation of the Qur'ān, I believe that a multicultural global village should be the starting point for a discussion of human rights. The Qur'ān is extremely conscious of its own history, and Muslim exegetes have developed tools to understand the verses in their specific historical contexts. With globalization, the basic social and political contexts have changed. In fact, the world has physically changed to an extent unimaginable to the early commentators of the Qur'ān and Islamic jurisprudence. There is a desperate need for no less than a radical revision of the moral foundations of a global village, and Muslims do not have the luxury of staying out of the debate. It sometimes appears that some Muslims are happy to demand freedoms and rights to practise Islam in every part of the globe, but hide behind cultural uniqueness when it applies to conferring rights on others. The case of schisms like the Ahmadis in Pakistan or the Baha'is in Iran exhibits this opportunistic approach to rights. Muslims seem only to confirm their own marginal status by continually demanding rights, in contrast with days gone by when they were the ones who were expected to grant rights to others. This does not mean that Muslims must simply accommodate themselves to the demands of individualistic Western culture and its particular understanding of human rights. Globalization has placed communities, religious and cultural, in the spotlight, whereas modernization and secularization had favoured the individual. Thus, the experience and history of minority religions in Islamic history provide foundations for inspiration. The *millet* system of the Ottoman empire, for example, should be the subject of reflection, both for its successes and its failures, in relation to shaping the meaning of rights and duties in a global world. In this way, Muslims may be able to contribute positively to the human rights debate, instead of taking the protective, reactionary positions which seem the order of the day.

Freedom of conscience is one of the fundamental rights that ought to be the subject of deep reflection by Muslims at the end of the twentieth century. If we keep in mind the nature of modern society, then other rights must equally receive the attention of Muslims. Gender rights and freedom of speech, as well as the social rights to basic necessities, provide opportunities to make a difference. The most important principle to keep in mind is the nature of the challenge: to build a foundation for the development of individuals and societies in a global village. As Sachedina has pointed out, freedom of conscience lies at the heart of this quest. 'Truth stands out from error' is the declaration of the Qur'ān rejecting coercion and promoting truth, dignity and justice.

There should be no illusion that human rights in a particular context may not become embroiled in local struggles. Like all good symbols and ethical values, human rights are subject to use and abuse by a variety of political actors. There may be groups who oppose human rights in order to protect vested interests, and not only because the concept of rights is incompatible with a particular culture. The supposed cultural conflict may be used in order to protect vested interests. Likewise, the demands for human rights can be very selectively employed in relation to friends and enemies. Hence, for example, the abuse of human rights in Israel receives much less coverage in the United States than human rights violations in Saudi Arabia. And human rights abuses in Saudi Arabia, in turn, can be forgotten or ignored compared with such abuses in Iraq or Sudan. The assessment of human rights is exposed to the vagaries of political interests and human frailty. In spite of these pitfalls, however, the concept of human rights as the foundation of a multicultural society may be the only measure by which to establish and judge the basic dignity and rights befitting every human *qua* human on the planet. We may guard against the abuse of human rights for ulterior motives, but we cannot afford to ignore the idea of a benchmark of the minimal worth of all individuals.

SYMBOL AND REALITY

The third and final section of this chapter explores the continuing validity of the religious dimension of Islam in the global village. The urgency of the question cannot be denied, precisely because religion takes an important place in public life. What is the unique contribution of a religion such as Islam that distinguishes it from other social and political philosophies? If justice, equity and morality are the criteria by which a human rights culture is founded, does it mean that religion simply helps people to acquire such values? Or is there something unique within Islam in particular and religion in general with which it can enrich the global village? In order to appreciate such a dimension, I think we ought to begin by understanding how different Muslims have posited the unique essence of Islam. This will be followed by a consideration of their views in the light of what I call the symbolization of religion at the end of the twentieth century.

I have repeatedly tried to highlight the fact that, in a variety of contexts and despite contrary appearances, Islam is in a state of change. Under the impact of social transformations such as colonialism, European Enlightenment philosophy, industrialization, and now globalization, it is short-sighted to ignore the change and transformation of Islam. Some of the leading Muslim intellectuals have tried to come to grips with such a transformation and to steer Islam in a particular direction. They are far from unanimous, but there is no doubt that, across political and religious divides, Muslims have been grappling with the challenges of the twentieth century. By paying careful attention to their ideas and proposals for Islam, we can better appreciate what the role of Islam as religion at the turn of a new century may be. In this section I present the seminal ideas of Rahman, Al Fārūqī, and Nasr. None of them advocates the end of religion in the modern world, but they differ considerably as to how and what Islam should be.

The Pakistani scholar Fazlur Rahman (d. 1988) has become one of the most prominent symbols of Islamic modernism. By this I mean that he saw himself in the trajectory of nineteenth-century reformist thinkers who tried to reformulate Islam in terms of science, constitutionalism and freedom. This particular trend has lost much favour among Muslims, who regard it as extremely apologetic towards the West. Rahman himself had critical comments about this kind of modernism, but he still maintained that the Islamic world could learn a great deal from Western critical approaches to modern issues. In fact, he believed that the Islamic tradition itself contained the resources for the redefinition of Islam that was taking place in modern critical scholarship. Muslims, according to Rahman, must recover that tradition.

Rahman appealed to Muslims to read the early texts of Islam in order to understand a 'message that will enable those who have faith in it and want to live by its guidance – in both their individual and collective lives – to do so coherently and meaningfully' (Rahman 1982: 4). He was acutely aware of historical change, and rejected the wholesale duplication of Islamic social forms in the modern world. Thus, as early as 1965, he argued in *Islamic Methodology in History* that the social forms of early Islam were 'absolutely irrepeatable' since the earliest Muslims also approached the Qur'ān and the *sunnah* in a creative manner:

> if we are able to live as progressive Muslims at all, viz., just as those generations met their own situation adequately by freely interpreting the Qur'ān and Sunnah of the Prophet – by emphasizing the ideal and the principles and re-embodying them in a fresh texture of their own contemporary history – we must perform the same feat ourselves, with our own effort, for our own contemporary history.
>
> (Rahman 1965: 178)

Rahman believed quite passionately that it was the responsibility of Muslim scholars to search for the principles and values that lay at the heart of Islamic teachings, and that the capacity to understand was absolutely essential for such a venture. In this regard, he rejected a trend within Muslim society simply to repeat what had been done in the past, as well as a trend within Western philosophy that questioned the possibility of objective understanding. Clearly, he was not a blind imitator of either the Islamic legacy or contemporary Western philosophy.

For Rahman, the key elements of the 'original experience of Muhammad' were the absolute belief in one God and the Last Day, and the implementation of socio-economic justice. These fundamental principles should guide Muslims in conducting their lives in a period of intense change. Rahman was keen to exclude the formal religious duties, but he felt the social and political norms of early Islam must be subject to change in the light of these principles. Thus he believed that issues such as women's rights, and interfaith relations, must be guided by these principles. Particular practices in early Islamic history should not be regarded as eternally binding upon Muslims. Given the capacity of human beings to understand the Qur'ān and the purpose and principles intended therein, Muslims can venture to reform their societies.

This particular approach did not mean that Rahman was succumbing to the pressures of secularization, modernity or the West. According to Rahman, the fundamental principle of Islam facilitated moral action in the world (Rahman 1982: 13, 14). And moral action, based on principles of accountability and justice, elevated human action above the mundane and the ordinary. Moral action was testimony to the reality of extra-historical and transcendental being (Rahman 1982: 5). Proper moral action was not possible in the absence of religious and transcendental faith. It is not surprising, therefore, that Rahman identified the root problem of modernity as its secularism which 'destroyed the sanctity and universality (transcendence) of all moral values' (Rahman 1982: 15).

Against secularism, moral action enabled Muslims to transform the world and human society to reflect the values of justice and equity.

The second scholar who saw the need for the continuing validity of Islam in the modern world was Ismā'īl Rājī al Fārūqī (d. 1986). He was an activist scholar who sought to make Islam a viable way of life for Muslims in the modern world. He sometimes seemed to be rejecting modernity, and sometimes endorsing it. Al Fārūqī's work on Islam includes an essay on Islam (1974) as part of an anthology of world religions, an introduction to Islam (1979), and finally a comprehensive work entitled *The Cultural Atlas of Islam* (1986). The last-mentioned book was produced with his wife shortly before their brutal, untimely death. In some respects, al Fārūqī came close to endorsing Rahman, particularly on Islamic law about which he said:

> the law acknowledged, futher, that the law is susceptible to change in time and place, conditioned as it must be by the status quo of the addressees. The needs of various societies must determine the nature of the laws they may be expected to observe. The principles of the law and its ends, on the other hand, stand above change and must remain the same throughout creation, since they represent the ultimate purposes of the Creator.
>
> (Al Fārūqī and al Fārūqī 1986: 108)

Like Rahman, al Fārūqī stressed the underlying principles of Islam. However, whereas Rahman focused on religious and socio-political principles of revelation, al Fārūqī was concerned about the importance of sound, rational theological and philosophical foundations. The central essence of Islam, according to al Fārūqī, was *tawḥīd*, the affirmation of the oneness of God. This was not a simply numeral unity, but encompassed 'a general view of reality, of truth, of the world, of space and time, of human history' (al Fārūqī and al Fārūqī 1986: 74). As the essence of Islam, *tawḥīd* led to important consequences in the belief system that informed its worldview. Against the mystics, al Fārūqī insisted on the utter and absolute difference between God and creation. This did not mean that humankind was therefore robbed of its capacity to transcend its material existence. Humankind was not condemned to the here and now, to the material existence of food, clothing and shelter. Rather, endowed with the capacity of reason, humankind could understand reality, its basic purpose, and its subservience to manipulation. It had the capacity to transform nature, and produce moral virtue. And finally, *tawḥīd* implied that human action was answerable and accountable to God and to sound moral principles. Al Fārūqī was certainly not opposed to social justice, but this feature did not take centre stage in the principles of Islam. Hence, unlike Rahman, al Fārūqī did not focus on social reform, and appeared to be restating the basic beliefs of Islam in rational and a philosophical form. This restatement, however, was far from traditional. In fact, a close look at his theology reveals its modernism:

> Through *tawḥīd*, therefore, nature was separated from the gods and spirits of primitive religion. *Tawḥīd* for the first time made it possible for the religio-mythopoeic mind to outgrow itself, for the sciences of nature and civilisation to develop with the blessing of a religious worldview that renounced once and for all any association of the sacred with nature. *Tawḥīd* is the opposite of superstition or myth, the enemies of natural science and civilisation.
>
> (Al Fārūqī and al Fārūqī 1986: 80)

In this sense, one can clearly see how the author has completely restated the meaning of Islam for the twentieth century. He endorsed a form of social evolution that became popular at the end of the nineteenth century, in which religion was regarded as an important milestone to scientific discovery. Al Fārūqī's view of Islam has eliminated the magical and mythical dimensions of the religion, and produced a rationalized theology amenable to science and progress. The essence of Islam, therefore, was the rational theology of *tawḥīd*.

Another prominent Muslim intellectual who has written extensively about Islam in the second half of the twentieth century is Seyyed Hossein Nasr. Unlike Rahman and al Fārūqī, Nasr completely rejects modernity and modernization. He re-asserts the relevance of the philosophical and intellectual tradition of pre-modern Islam. Discussing the meaning of contemporary art, Nasr attacks its propensity to see 'the origin of the inward in the outward and [to] reduce sacred art with its interiorizing power to simply external, social and, in the Marxist historians, economic conditions' (Nasr 1990: 4). For Nasr, what was true of art was also true of modern philosophy, not to speak of the social sciences and humanities. This characterization of modernity is, to a degree, similar to Al Fārūqī's analysis of it. Nasr, however, also rejects the rationalism of the Enlightenment, which both al Fārūqī and Rahman accepted to a certain extent, finding the human-centred rationality of the Enlightenment equally problematic from an Islamic perspective. He does not see the utility of the Enlightenment's practical reason and moral values that both Rahman and al Fārūqī endorse.

For Nasr, the essence of Islam lies in its mystical dimension. Islam is the 'direct call of the Absolute to man inviting him to cease his wandering in the labyrinth of the relative and to return to the Absolute and the One; it appeals to what is most permanent and immutable in man' (Nasr 1991: 148). The true purpose of Islam is not the establishment of social justice (Rahman), nor the establishment of Islam as a rational civilisation (al Fārūqī), but the recovery of one's true inner, primordial nature. Nasr goes further and evaluates this inner dimension in relation to other religious traditions. Accordingly, absolute truth is inherent in all religious traditions. Like all other religions, however, Islam contains both an absolute and a relative dimension. According to Nasr, Islam 'contains within itself the Truth and means of attaining the Truth' but as a historical religion, it 'emphasises a particular aspect of the Truth in conformity with the spiritual and psychological needs of the humanity for whom it is destined and to whom it is addressed' (Nasr 1994: 15). Each religious tradition 'emphasises certain aspect of this relationship, while inwardly it contains the Truth as such in its teachings whatever the outward limitations of its forms might be' (Nasr 1994: 16). When Nasr alerts us to the 'psychological needs of humanity' we recall Rahman and al Fārūqī on the changing nature of specific forms. However, Nasr would have none of that. The relative dimension of religions does not pertain to practices within a particular religious tradition. Practices that may have been endorsed in the second century of Islam do not necessarily have to change in the twentieth century, as Rahman and al Fārūqī would argue. He focuses only on the different forms of prayer and worship in Christianity and Islam, for example. In each religious tradition, Nasr insists on the efficacy of the forms of religious life as vehicles, ultimate symbols, through which the Absolute may be attained. The Qur'ān, the *Sharī'ah* and practical behaviour of the Prophet are all the authentic means, pure symbols of reaching inwardness. In the pursuit of inwardness, Nasr has no clear views on the issues of social justice and public morality that dominate Rahman.

The search for purity and ultimate essence within religion, has, it seems, produced different results. Rahman, al Fārūqī and Nasr seem to have been searching for some underlying core of the tradition. Rahman and al Fārūqī searched for a redefinition and reconfiguration of Muslim social space. Rahman posited moral action to defy secularism; al Fārūqī posited the demystification of nature. Although openly anti-secularist, they both carried the seed of secular thought. In spite of their different political views, moreover, both articulated Islam for the twentieth century. Nasr's appeal to the primordial tradition rejects modernity, but the quest for stability and the moderation of his views on social reform as a religious concern are effects of modernity on religion. Science and humanism provided a solution to everything but the primordial nature of human life, which the inwardness of Islam and other traditional religions can provide. In spite of the rejection of modernity, partly or wholly, it seems that the search for the principles or the core becomes urgent precisely as a result of the effects of modernity. Modernity does not necessarily lead to complete secularization, but it certainly calls into question many of the functions and aspects of traditional religions. The redefinition, or at least the recovery, of the core of Islam in the twentieth century underlines the need to adjust and respond comprehensively and coherently to Islam in the modern world.

The search for the core of Islam, is, it seems, urgent and necessary. In this regard, I believe that one also needs to appreciate the inherently symbolic dimension of religions. Islam, like all other religions, necessarily contains a symbolic dimension at many levels. Reference to God, who is indescribable and inexpressible, must be made in symbolic language. This has been the symbolism of Islam at a traditional level. Classical scholarship, therefore, developed the notion of *majāz* (allegory) to understand religious texts as well as to speak of God using human language. The concept of *majāz* referred to the inherently approximate, inherently deficient nature of all words, events and phenomena used as symbols to refer to the Ultimate.

The symbolic nature of religion in the modern world, however, has been magnified. As science, philosophy and politics pursued aspects previously regarded as the preserve of religion, the latter's symbolic potential has been modified and compounded. Now, religious symbols are not restricted to the Ineffable and the Ultimate: they also provide a convenient way of referring to other aspects of religion. To take one example, in the Islamic tradition, rain clouds were the responsibility of specially assigned angels. With the advent of meteorology, these angels and their function have had to be reformulated, discarded, or simply left to co-exist with each other. In each case, the meaning of the angels of rain becomes open to a more complex degree of symbolization. Where previously, angels may have been regarded as a form of reality, they now may better be understood and appropriated as symbols of the beneficence and grace of God. In spite of the persistence of religion at the end of twentieth century, then, its beliefs and values are open to multiple levels of symbolic assignment. Where once religious symbols explained reality, they now stand for the belief systems of religious communities. Needless to say, the latter case exhibits a greater degree of variation.

The symbolization of religion continues as a framework for explaining reality. Now, however, this reality is determined by social and political struggles for nationalism, ethnicity, identity and authenticity, to name the most prominent. As Muslims engage religion in the public arena, their non-religious codes are intermeshed with Islamic ones. From the tomb of Khomeini in Iran, to women's dress codes, to ethnic struggles, Islamic symbols construct a new reality for Muslims in the modern world. Veiling, for example, may refer to the complete negation of women's role in public life, as well as to their assertiveness in a male-dominated polity (Eickelman and Piscatori 1996: 90). Women employ the symbol of veiling in unexpected ways, different from both the traditional and the modern meaning of female seclusion. We may, thus, speak most appropriately about the *islams* of individuals and groups who use the opportunities of modernity and globalization to determine their relationship with Islam in varied contexts. In spite of Muslim intellectual insistence that the essence of Islam is moral, civilizational or mystical, we must expect otherwise. Modernity has broken the link between religion and representation in fundamental ways. Sometimes, the symbolic appropriation of Islam may also be patriarchal, ethnic or personal, and the particular appropriation of the symbol of Islam can only be appreciated and grappled with if one understands how such symbols are employed creatively in social contexts.

It would appear from the foregoing that the symbolization of religion would lead necessarily to a postmodernist continuous play of symbols and referents. As soon as one gives up the essentialist quests conducted by Rahman, al Fārūqī or Nasr, it seems that one is left completely adrift in a maelstrom of symbols. This need not be so. There is a difference between the meaning of a particular symbol or set of symbols of Islam as studied by observers, and the symbolism seen from a religious perspective. The scientific study of religion has extensively studied the first, and pointed out the social and individual significance of religion in the modern world. Power, community and individual fears and hopes reveal themselves through the religious expressions of myth, ritual and symbols. However, symbolism within a religion like Islam is different from these. When reflected upon by religious people, the symbolism of Islam as a reference to ultimacy is both temporary and purposive. It is temporary because it is part of a journey that continually seeks to transcend the stations. Each symbolic appropriation of Islam may be thought of as a station, a goal on the religious quest which must be transcended on the journey to the Ultimate. When the veil is appropriated for a return to tradition or the assertion of women's place in a male-dominated society, neither can become an end in itself. The religious quest must continue, just as the quest to seek the Ultimate may not be arrested at a particular station. At this level, the religious quest may have something in common with the postmodernist suspicion of fixed places. However, it goes beyond this continuous play, with the conviction that the journey must still go on in a purposive direction. Here, it leaves postmodernism behind. It must be admitted that not all religious people appreciate and accept the temporary nature of symbolization. This does not mean, however, that such a possibility should be discarded on principle. For Muslims, the temporary nature of symbolization cannot be ignored.

In conclusion, then, the meaning of Islam at the end of the twentieth century would have to be a highly symbolic quest that finds its essence in a personal or social venture. Muslims across the globe will necessarily draw on a rich history to make sense of their particular social and individual locations, resulting in a highly symbolic appropriation of the resources of Islam and modern life. There are two conditions for such an appropriation. First, the symbolic appropriation will have seriously to grapple with the responsibilities and opportunities of living in the global village. The priorities of human rights, or the sanctity of the earth as a natural environment, will not be sacrificed for a religious symbol. Second, the appropriation of Islamic symbols will have to heed the lesson of the early Sufi masters. If symbolization remains locked at any one level, on one station as it were, then it will be a caricature of the transcendence exemplified in the Qur'ān.

BIBLIOGRAPHY

Abdali, S. K. 1997. 'The Correct Qiblah'. Internet Paper. Http://www.patriot.net/users/abdali/ftp/qiblah.pdf:20 pp.

Abdel-Kader, A. H. 1962. *The Life, Personality and Writings of al-Junayd: A Study of a Third/Ninth-Century Mystic With an Edition and Translation of his Writings*. E. J. W. Gibb Memorial Series. London: Luzac & Co.

Abdel-Rahim, M. 1980. 'Legal Institutions'. In *The Islamic City*, ed. R. B. Sergeant, 41–51. Paris: Unesco.

Andrae, T. 1987. *In the Garden of the Myrtles: Studies in Early Islamic Mysticism,* trans. B. Sharpe. Foreword by A. Schimmel. SUNY Series in Muslim Spirituality in South Asia. Albany: State University of New York Press.

Antoun, R. T. 1989. *Muslim Preacher in the Modern World*. Princeton: Princeton University Press.

Arberry, A. J. (trans.) 1968. *Mystical Poems of Rūmī, First Selection: Poems 1–200.* Persian Heritage Series. Chicago: University of Chicago Press.

Arkoun, M. 1994. *Rethinking Islam: Common Questions, Uncommon Answers,* trans. R. D. Lee. Boulder: Westview Press.

Asad, M. 1980. *The Message of the Qur'ān*. Gibraltar: Dar al-Andalus.

Asad, T. 1986. *The Idea of an Anthropology of Islam*. Occasional Papers Series. Washington, DC: Center for Contemporary Arab Studies, Georgetown University.

—— 1993. *Genealogies of Religion: Discipline and Reasons of Power in Christianity and Islam*. Baltimore: Johns Hopkins University Press.

Askari, H. 1985. 'Within and Beyond the Experience of Religious Diversity'. In *The Experience of Religious Diversity*, ed. by H. Askari and J. Hick, 191–218. Avebury Series in Philosophy: Gower.

Ayoub, M. 1988. 'The Speaking Qur'an and the Silent Qur'an: A Study of the Principles and Development of Imami Shi'i Tafsīr'. In *Approaches to the History of the Interpretation of the Qur'an*, ed. A. Rippin, 177–98. Oxford: Clarendon Press.

Azami, M. M. 1977. *Studies in Ḥadīth Methodology and Literature*. Indianapolis: American Trust Publications.

Al-Azmeh, A. 1993. *Islams and Modernities*. London: Verso.

Beckford, J. 1992. 'Religion, Modernity and Post-modernity'. In *Religion: Contemporary Issues*, ed. B. Wilson, 11–23. London: Bellew Publishing.

Berger, M. 1970. *Islam in Egypt Today: Social and Political Aspects of Popular Religion*. Cambridge: Cambridge University Press.

Biersteker, A. 1991. 'Language, Poetry, and Power: A Reconsideration of "Utendi wa Mwana Kupona"'. In *Faces of Islam in African Literature*, ed. K. W. Harrow, 59–77. London: James Currey.

Bloom, J. 1989. *Minaret: Symbol of Islam*. Oxford: Oxford University Press.

Chidester, D. 1992. *Shots in the Streets: Violence and Religion in South Africa*. Contemporary South African Debates. Cape Town: Oxford University Press.

Chittick, W. C. 1983. *The Sufi Path of Love: The Spiritual Teachings of Rumi*. Albany: State University of New York Press.

Clasquin, M. 1993. 'Buddhism and Human Rights'. *Journal for the Study of Religion*, 6(2): 91–101.

Crone, P. and M. Hinds. 1986. *God's Caliph: Religious Authority in the First Centuries of Islam*. Cambridge: Cambridge University Press.

Douglas, M. 1970. *Purity and Danger: An Analysis of Concepts of Pollution and Taboo*. London: Pelican Books.

Eickelman, D. F. 1985. *Knowledge and Power in Morocco: The Education of a Twentieth-Century Noble*. Princeton: Princeton University Press.

Eickelman, D. F. and J. Piscatori. 1996. *Muslim Politics*. Princeton: Princeton University Press.

Enayat, H. 1982. *Modern Islamic Political Thought*. Austin: University of Texas Press.

Evans-Pritchard, E. E. 1949. *The Sanusi of Cyrenaica*. Oxford: Clarendon Press.

al Fārūqī, I. R. 1974. 'Islam'. In *Historical Atlas of the Religions of the World*, ed. I. R. al Fārūqī and D. E. Sopher, 237–81. New York: Macmillan.

—— 1979. *Islam*. Major World Religions Series. Allen, Texas: Argus Communications.

al Fārūqī, I. R. and L. L. al Fārūqī. 1986. *The Cultural Atlas of Islam*. London and New York: Macmillan.

al Fārūqī, L. L. 1985. *Islam and Art*. Islamabad: National Hijra Council.

Fisher, H. J. 1973. 'Conversion Reconsidered: Some Historical Aspects of Religious Conversion in Black Africa'. *Africa: Journal of the International African Institute*, 43(1): 27–40.

Geertz, C. 1968. *Islam Observed: Religious Development in Morocco and Indonesia*. The Dwight Harrington Terry Foundation Lectures on Religion in the Light of Science and Philosophy. New Haven: Yale University Press.

Gellner, E. 1981. *Muslim Society*. Cambridge Studies in Social Anthropology. Cambridge: Cambridge University Press.

Al-Ghazālī, Abū Ḥāmid Muḥammad (1085–1111). 1964. *The Alchemy of Happiness*, trans. from Hindustani to English by C. Field. Lahore: Ashraf Press.

al-Ghazālī, M. 1989. *al-Sunnah al-nabawiyyah bayn ahl al-fiqh wa ahl al-ḥadīth* (The Prophetic model between jurists and *ḥadith* scholars). Cairo: Dār al-Shurūq.

Gilsenan, M. 1990. *Recognizing Islam: Religion and Society in the Modern Middle East*. New York and London: I. B. Tauris.

Goldziher, I. 1971. *Muslim Studies*, ed. S. M. Stern, trans. C. R. Barber and S. M. Stern. 2 vols. London: George Allen & Unwin.

Graham, W. A. 1983. 'Islam in the Mirror of Ritual'. In *Islam's Understanding of Itself*, ed. R. G. Hovannisian and S. Vryonis. Malibu: Undena Publications.

Hamidullah, M. 1968. *The First Written Constitution in the World: An Important Document of the Time of the Holy Prophet*. Lahore: Sh. Muhammad Ashraf.

Hamidullah, M. (comp.) 1969. *Majmūʿat al-wathā'iq al-siyāsiyyah li 'l-ahd al-nabawī wa 'l-khilāfah al-rāshidah* (Collection of political documents from the Prophetic and righteous caliphate periods). Beirut: Dār al-irshād.

Hermansen, M. 1996. *The Conclusive Argument from God: Shah Wali Allah of Delhi's 'Hujjat Allah al-Balighah'*. Leiden: E. J. Brill.

al-Ḥilli, Jamāl al-Dīn al-Ḥasan b. Yūsuf 'Alī b. Muṭahhar (d. 1325). n. d. *Tadhkirat al-fuqahā'* (The reminder to the jurists). n. p.: Maktabah al-Murtaḍawiyyah Li Iḥyā' al-āthār al-Ja'fariyyah.

Hodgson, M. G. S. 1974. *The Venture of Islam: Conscience and History in a World Civilization*. Chicago: Chicago University Press.

Huntingdon, S. P. 1996. *The Clash of Civilizations and the Remaking of the World Order*. New York: Simon & Schuster.

Ibn al-'Arabī al-Mālikī (1165–1240). n.d. 'Āriḍah al-Aḥwadhī bisharḥ Ṣaḥīḥ al-Tirmidhī' (The demonstration of the knowledgeable: explanation of *Ṣaḥiḥ Tirmidhī*). Cairo: Dār al-Fikr.

Ibn Ḥajar 'Asqalānī, Aḥmad b. 'Alī (1371–1448). n.d. *Fatḥ al-Bārī bi Sharḥ Saḥīḥ al-Imām Abī 'Abd Allah Muḥammad b. Ismā'īl al-Bukhārī (d. 870)* (The opening of the latent field), ed. Muḥammad Fu'ād 'Abd al-Bāqī. Cairo: al-Maktabah al-Salafiyyah.

Ibn Khaldūn, 'Abd al-Raḥmān b. Muḥammad (1332–1406). n. d. *Muqaddimah Ibn Khaldūn* (The prolegomena of Ibn Khaldūn). Beirut: Dār Jīl.

Ibn Mājah, Muḥammad b. Yazīd al-Qazwīnī (824–87). n.d. *Sunan al-Ḥafīẓ Abū 'Abd Allah Muḥammad b. Yazīd al-Qazwīnī* (Prophetic practice according to Abū 'Abd Allah Muḥammad b. Yazīd), ed. Fu'ād 'Abd al-Bāqī. Cairo: Halabi.

Ibn Qudāmah, Abī Muḥammad 'Abd Allah b. Aḥmad b. Muḥammad (1146–1223). 1968. *al-Mughnī 'alā mukhtaṣar Abī al-Qāsim 'Umar b. Ḥusayn b. 'Abd Allah b. Aḥmad al-Kharqī (d. 334H)* (The sufficient [explanation] on the summary of Abū al-Qāsim 'Umar b. Ḥusayn b. 'Abd Allah b. Aḥmad al-Kharqī), ed. Ṭahā Muḥammad al-Zayni. Cairo: Maktabah al-Qāhirah.

Ibn Rushd, Abū al-Walīd Muḥammad b. Aḥmad (1126–98). n.d. *Fasl al-maqāl fīmā bayn al-ḥikmah wa 'l-sharī'ah min 'l-ittiṣāl* (The decisive treatise concerning the connection between philosophy and legal doctrine), ed. Muḥammad 'Imārah. Cairo: Dār al-Ma'ārif.

Jamiat ul Ulema. 1981. *Kitaabut Tahaarah* (The book of purification [Hanafi]). Benoni, South Africa: Jamiat ul Ulema.

al-Jazā'irī, 'Abd al-Raḥmān. n.d. *Kitāb al-fiqh 'alā al-madhāhib al-arba'ah* (Jurisprudence according to the four schools of thought). Cairo: Dār al-Fikr.

Jeffreys, A. (ed.) 1962. *A Reader on Islam: Passages from Standard Arabic Writing Illustrative of the Beliefs and Practices of Muslims*. The Hague: Mouton & Co.

al-Jīlānī, Shaikh 'Abd al-Qādir (1077–1166). 1995. *Sufficient Provision for Seekers of the Path of Truth (al-Ghunya li-ṭālib ṭarīq al-ḥaqq): A Complete Resource on the Inner and Outer Aspects of Islam,* trans. M. Holland. Hollywood, FL: Al-Baz Publishing.

Kaptein, N. 1993. *Muḥammad's Birthday Festival: Early History in the Central Lands in the Muslim West until the 10th/16th Century.* Leiden: E. J. Brill.

Khomeini, Ayatollah Sayyed Ruhollah Mousavi. 1985. *The Practical Laws of Islam: An Abridged Version of 'Taudih-al-Masa'il'*. 2nd edn. Tehran: n. p.

Kinghorn, J. 1991. 'Human Rights and the Contribution of Religion in the Shaping of a New South African Community'. Presentation to the conference 'The Contribution of South African Religions to the Coming South Africa', University of Natal, Pietermaritzburg, Natal, 15–17 September.

Lambek, M. 1990. 'Certain Knowledge, Contestable Authority: Power and Practice on the Islamic Periphery'. *American Ethnologist: The Journal of the American Ethnological Society,* 17: 23–40.

Laoust, H. 1960. 'Aḥmad b. Ḥanbal'. In *Encyclopedia of Islam,* 2nd edn. Leiden: E. J. Brill.

Lapidus, I. M. 1967. *Muslim Cities in the Later Middle Ages.* Harvard: Harvard University Press.

Leila, A. 1992. *Women and Gender in Islam: Historical Roots of a Modern Debate.* New Haven: Yale University Press.

Lewis, B. 1966 (1964). *The Middle East and the West.* New York: Harper & Row.

Lings, M. 1983. *Muhammad: His Life Based on the Earliest Sources.* 3rd edn. India: Islamic Book Printers.

Little, D., J. Kelsay and A. A. Sachedina. 1988. *Human Rights and the Conflict of Cultures: Western and Islamic Perspectives on Religious Liberty.* Columbia, SC: University of South Carolina Press.

Mahmoud, M. 1996. 'The Discourse of the Ikhwān of Sudan and Secularism'. In *Questioning the Secular State: The Worldwide Resurgence of Religion in Politics,* ed. D. Westerlund, 167–82. London: Hurst & Co.

Martin, R. C., M. R. Woodward and D. S. Atmaja. 1997. *Defenders of Reason in Islam: Mu'tazilism from Medieval School to Modern Symbol.* Oxford: Oneworld.

Massignon, L. 1982 (1975). *The Passion of al-Ḥallāj: Mystic and Martyr of Islam,* ed. and trans. H. Mason. Bollingen Series, 98. Princeton: Princeton University Press.

Masud, M. K. 1996. 'Apostacy and Judicial Separation in British India'. In *Islamic Legal Interpretation: Muftis and their Fatwas,* ed. M. K. Masud, B. Messick and D. S. Powers, 193–203. Cambridge, MA: Harvard University Press.

Mernissi, F. 1991. *Women and Islam: An Historical and Theological Enquiry,* trans. M. J. Lakeland. Oxford: Blackwell Publishers.

Metcalf, B. D. 1995. 'Deoband'. In *Oxford Encyclopedia of the Modern Islamic World,* ed. J. Esposito. New York: Oxford University Press.

Momen, M. 1985. *An Introduction to Shi'i Islam: The History and Doctrines of Twelver Shi'ism.* New Haven and London: Yale University Press.

Moosa, E. 1991. 'Religion and Human Rights: Taking Rights Religiously'. Presentation to the conference 'The Contribution of South African Religions to the Coming South Africa', University of Natal, Pietermaritzburg, Natal, 15–17 September.

El Moudden, A. 1990. 'The Ambivalence of Rihla: Community Integration and Self-Definition in Moroccan Travel Accounts, 1300–1800'. In *Muslim Travellers: Pilgrimage, Migration and the Religious Imagination*, ed. D. F. Eickelman and J. Piscatori, 69–84. Comparative Studies on Muslim Societies, 9. Berkeley: University of California Press.

Nasr, S. H. 1990. *Islamic Art and Spirituality.* Delhi: Oxford University Press.

—— 1991. *Sufi Essays.* 2nd edn. Albany: State University of New York Press.

—— 1994. *Ideals and Realities of Islam.* London: HarperCollins.

An-Nawawi, Yaḥyā b. Sharaf al-Dīn (1233–77), 1976. *An-Nawawi's Forty Hadith*, trans. E. Ibrahim and D. Johnson-Davies. Damascus: The Holy Koran Publishing House.

Nelson, K. 1985. *The Art of Reciting the Qur'ān.* Austin: University of Texas Press.

Newby, G. D. 1989. *The Making of the Last Prophet.* Columbia, SC: University of South Carolina Press.

Paret, R. 1991 (1957). *Mohammed und der Koran: Geschichte und Verkündigung des arabischen Propheten.* 7th edn. Stuttgart: Verlag W. Kohlhammer.

Pearson, M. N. 1994. *Pious Passengers: The Hajj in Earlier Times.* London: Hurst & Co.

Pellat, C. (ed. and trans.) 1969. *The Life and Works of Jāḥiẓ: Translations of Selected Texts*, trans. from the French D. M. Hawke. The Islamic World Series. London: Routledge & Kegan Paul.

Peters, F. E. 1994. *The Hajj: The Muslim Pilgrimage to Mecca and the Holy Places.* Princeton: Princeton University Press.

Prozesky, M. 1989. 'Is the Concept of Human Rights Logically Permissible in Theistic Religion?', *Journal for the Study of Religion*, 2(2): 17–26.

al-Qurtubī, 'Abd Allah Muḥammad b. Aḥmad al-Anṣārī (d. 1272). 1967. *al-Jāmi' li aḥkām al-qur'ān* (The collection for the laws of the Qur'an). Cairo: n. p.

Qutb, S. 1980. *Fīẓilāl al-qur'ān* (In the shades of the Qur'ān). Cairo: Dār al-Shurūq.

Rahman, F. 1958. *Prophecy in Islam: Philosophy and Orthodoxy.* Midway Reprint. Chicago and London: University of Chicago Press.

—— 1965. *Islamic Methodology in History.* Karachi: Central Institute of Islamic Research.

—— 1982. *Islam and Modernity: Transformation of an Intellectual Tradition.* Chicago: University of Chicago Press.

Reinhart, A. K. 1990. 'Impurity/No Danger'. *History of Religions* 30(1): 1–24.

Sābiq, S. 1980. *Fiqh al-sunnah* (Jurisprudence the Prophetic model). 2nd edn. Beirut: Dār al-Fikr.

Salvatore, A. 1997. *Islam and the Political Discourse of Modernity.* Reading, Berkshire: Ithaca Press.

Schimmel, A. 1985. *And Muhammad is His Messenger.* Chapel Hill and London: University of North Carolina Press.

Shafī', Muftī M. (1963). *Ālāt jadīdah ke aḥkām shar'ī* (The Islamic legal rule concerning new technology). Deoband, India: Kutub Khānah Qāsimī.

Shariati, A. 1980. *Hajj,* ed. and trans. A. A. Behzadnia and N. Denny. 2nd edn. Houston: Free Islamic Literatures.

Ṣiddīqī, 'Abd al-Ḥamīd. 1976. *Ṣaḥīḥ Muslim: Being Traditions of the Sayings and Doings of the Prophet Muḥammad as Narrated by his Companions and Compiled Under the Title 'al-Jāmi' al-Ṣaḥīḥ' by Imam Muslim (d. 875)* 4 vols. Lahore: Sh. Muhammad Ashraf.

Ṣiddīqī, M. Z. 1961. *Ḥadīth Literature: Its Origins, Development, Special Features and Criticism.* Calcutta: Calcutta University Press.

Smith, M. 1928 (1984). *Rābi'a the Mystic and her Fellow-Saints in Islam: Being the Life and Teachings of Rābi'a al-'Adawiya al-Qaysiyya of Baṣra Together with Some Account of the Place of the Women Saints in Islam*. Cambridge: Cambridge University Press.

—— 1950. *Readings From the Mystics of Islam: Translations From the Arabic and Persian, Together with a Short Account of the History and Doctrines of Sufism and Brief Biographical Notes on each Sufi Writer.* London: Luzac & Co.

al-Ṭabarī, Abū Ja'far Muḥammad b. Jarīr (d. 923). 1879–1901. *Ta'rīkh al-rusul wa 'l-mulūk* (The history of prophets and kings), ed. M. J. De Goeje et al. Leiden: E. J. Brill.

Tapper, Nancy. 1990. Ziyaret: 'Gender, Movement, and Exchange in a Turkish Community'. In *Muslim Travellers: Pilgrimage, migration and the Religious Imagination*. Ed. D. F. Eickelman and J. Piscatori, 236–55. Comparative Studies on Muslim Societies, 9. Berkeley: University of California Press.

Tapper, N. and R. Tapper. 1987. 'The Birth of the Prophet: Ritual and Gender in Turkish Islam'. *Man*, New Series 22 (March): 69–92.

Turner, V. 1974. 'Pilgrimages as Social Processes'. In *Dramas, Fields, and Metaphors: Symbolic Action in Human Society*, ed. V. Turner, 166–230. Ithaca, NY: Cornell University Press.

'Ulwān, 'Abd Allāh Nāṣiḥ. 1981. *Tarbiyat al-awlād fi' al-Islām* (The education of children in Islam). 3rd edn. n. p.: Dār al-Salām.

Voll, J. O. 1982. *Islam: Continuity and Change in the Modern World.* Boulder: Westview Press.

Wilson, B. 1985. 'Secularization: The Inherited Model'. In *The Sacred in a Secular Age,* ed. P. E. Hammond, 9–20. Berkeley: University of California Press.

Wolfe, M. (ed.). 1997. *One Thousand Roads to Mecca: Ten Centuries of Travelers Writing about the Muslim Pilgrimage.* New York: Grove Press.

INDEX